DAVID C. KNIGHT

THE MOVING COFFINS
Ghosts and Hauntings Around the World

Illustrated by Neil Waldman

PRENTICE-HALL, INC.
Englewood Cliffs, New Jersey

Book design by Constance Ftera

Printed in the United States of America

Prentice-Hall International, Inc., London
Prentice-Hall of Australia, Pty. Ltd., Sydney
Prentice-Hall Canada, Inc., Toronto
Prentice-Hall of India Private Ltd., New Delhi
Prentice-Hall of Japan, Inc., Tokyo
Prentice-Hall of Southeast Asia Pte. Ltd., Singapore
Whitehall Books Limited, Wellington, New Zealand
Editoria Prentice-Hall Do Brasil LTDA., Rio de Janeiro

10 9 8 7 6 5 4 3 2 1

Library of Congress Cataloging in Publication Data

Knight, David C.
    The moving coffins.

    Includes index.
    Summary: Accounts of incidents in some twenty countries
around the world, involving poltergeists, apparitions,
and other supernatural manifestations.
    1. Ghosts—Juvenile literature. [1. Ghosts]
I. Waldman, Neil, ill.   II. Title.
BF1461.K594 1983   133.1   83-9447
ISBN 0-13-604645-2

CONTENTS

FOREWORD

THE GHOST STORIES IN THIS VOLUME ARE NOT FICTIONAL. They have no contrived plots, resolved conflicts, or satisfying endings. They are not intended to scare, chill, or frighten readers on a stormy night, or to be read aloud in anticipation of Halloween. Rather, they are offered as actual cases in psychical research, or parapsychology. Parapsychology is a division of psychology dealing with behavioral or personal effects that do not fall within the scope of known physical principles. This branch of science has a term for these stories: *spontaneous cases*. They are events that simply happened to people—unprompted and unbidden.

It is hoped that these case stories will serve a purpose beyond their entertainment value: to make readers aware that there are forces operating in dimensions beyond the cognizance of our five senses and that these forces can sometimes interact with our physical world in strange ways. To show that such forces are universal and not confined to one portion of the earth, the cases in this book have been selected from around the world, with all continents represented except Antarctica.

Parapsychologists—men and women who devote their lives to psychical research—know that so-called ghosts fall into two general categories: poltergeists and apparitions. Poltergeists are by far the most common ghostly phenomena, and many hundreds of cases have been reported. *Poltergeist* is a German word meaning "noisy ghost" or "racketing spirit." The true poltergeist is never seen; it is heard and occasionally felt, but only its effects can be witnessed. As unseen ghosts, poltergeists specialize in tossing crockery about, rapping and thumping, making crashing sounds, knocking on walls, and performing similar feats. In a strictly scientific sense, there is no such thing as a poltergeist—not as an actual entity or being. There are only poltergeist *activities* or poltergeist *disturbances*—curious events caused by some unknown force or power, possibly psychological in nature. Many poltergeist cases have been thoroughly investigated by trained researchers, who found that they could not be attributed to fraud, trickery, or natural causes.

Poltergeist activity can take place by day or by night, indoors or out. It can make objects move about in abnormal ways. The flying objects can sometimes hurt people, but they seldom do. There have been cases in which people have experienced ghostly forces touching them, lifting them, or sometimes slapping, pinching, pushing, or restraining them.

Poltergeist activity often announces its coming with certain "signal noises," such as rapping sequences, windlike sounds, or the lifting of door latches. It can also produce sounds that resemble those of humans, such as moaning, sighing, sobbing, screaming, and dragging footsteps. The events seem to run for a certain period of time: then they apparently lose their psychic energy and cease. In most cases, they go on for several weeks, but sometimes they have been known to last a year and more. Occasionally there have been visual effects involved, such as ghostly lights. The list of events poltergeists can cause is a long one. They can make pianos and organs play; rip clothing and yank off bedclothes; flip lights on and off; lock and unlock doors; steal keys; produce liquids such as milk or beer; suffuse rooms with perfumes; and perform a host of other activities.

Modern psychical researchers are deeply interested in poltergeist activity and what its ultimate meaning might be. In some cases, objects have appeared out of nowhere or have been thrown into or out of closed places. This implies the passing of physical matter through other physical matter—a seeming impossibility. It also involves *teleportation*; an object is said to be teleported if it is moved from one place to another by other than normal physical means.

Some theories have been proposed to account for these phenomena. One holds that the moving object is somehow first dematerialized or "dissolved" during teleportation, then rematerialized at the spot where it turns up and is seen by witnesses.

Another theory is based on the fact that much of physical matter is made up of empty space in its atomic structure; if the atoms of one object—say a brick wall—could be lined up exactly between those of another object—say a baseball— the ball could theoretically pass through the wall. But so far, atomic physics has not suggested how this might be done. Yet another theory involves the notion of a "fourth dimension"—a higher order of space that permits movement in some other, or "fourth," way that is different from the three-dimensional reality we are familiar with. However, modern science has yielded no evidence that such a dimension exists.

Parapsychologists have found that poltergeist activity tends to center around adolescent boys or girls who are approaching, undergoing, or have recently undergone puberty. Of course this is not always true—the disturbances can center around anyone at all—but it appears to be the general rule. Psychical researchers refer to them as "focus persons"; sometimes the activity follows these young people from one location to another. Often they are going through severe emotional stresses connected with blossoming sexual energies, of which they themselves may not be consciously aware. Researchers now are inclined to believe that in some manner these inner mental stresses may transfer themselves outside the body in the form of energy powerful enough to cause poltergeist disturbances.

Many parapsychologists also think that the phenomenon called *psychokinesis*—a term meaning the ability of mind-directed energy to move objects without any intermediate means—is associated with poltergeist activity. Psychokinesis, also popularly known as "mind over matter," is called PK for short. More often than not in poltergeist cases, the "focus" person is completely unaware that his own PK may be causing the activity. In any case, although PK has been proven to exist under controlled conditions in parapsychological laboratories, scientists still don't know what it really is or what makes it happen.

Checking out poltergeist cases is made more difficult because the disturbances don't last very long. Unless an investigator is on the spot when the events begin, or shortly afterward, his opportunity is gone. And sometimes the activity ceases completely in the presence of strangers or when the focus person or persons leave the scene. Moreover, the disturbances usually end as abruptly and unexpectedly as they started.

About the category of ghosts known as apparitions—phantoms, spirits, and the like that can actually be seen—even less is known. They are far less common than poltergeist cases. When seen by witnesses, such figures are usually wispy and transparent; often they glide rather than walk. They are seen only briefly and then either vanish or dissolve slowly from view. Photographs have been taken of apparitions, suggesting that at least some measure of physical matter—however thin its consistency—was present to register on the film's chemical emulsion.

In most cases, apparitions are of people known to be no longer living—a person or persons long dead or only recently dead. Of the latter, there is a body of cases known as "death-bed visions." In such cases, the spirit or apparition of a dying or recently deceased person appears to a loved one or friend, as if bidding a final affectionate farewell. In rare instances, two cases of which appear in this book, the apparition of a living person is seen, when that person is known to be somewhere else. These are called "double" cases. Also included in this book are some rather rare multiple-witness cases in which more than one observer sees the ghost. These are valuable because they confirm that the apparition is seen, whereas a single witness could be accused of hallucinating.

Parapsychology has not provided any real explanation of apparitional ghosts. Often they are simply classified as "visual hallucinations"—a seeming visual perception that has no objective reality. The "death-bed" visions are frequently written off as visual hallucinations. Something—no one knows just what—triggers the observer's sense of sight and he or she "sees," or believes that he or she sees, the apparition of the dead or dying person. But this is hardly a satisfactory answer.

Far more believable is the explanation offered by spiritualists and others, particularly followers of Eastern religions, that humans and indeed all living creatures survive the event known as physical death. They possess a second, or spirit, body—still material but highly attenuated and not usually visible to the human eye—that continues to exist after bodily death. Normally this second body passes to another dimensional plane where it takes up its new after-death life. But in some cases, newly dead persons—particularly those who have met violent deaths, perhaps by murder or in war—do not realize what has happened to them. In their new spirit bodies, which resemble the physical ones they have just shed, they are not aware that they have passed through physical death and they continue to linger about the places they have known in life. They are, according to this belief, "earthbound" and on occasion (no one can explain just how) their spirit bodies can materialize briefly as ghostly apparitions.

The spontaneous cases retold in these pages have come from a number of sources, including the *Journal* and *Proceedings* of the American Society for Psychical Research and publications of the British Society. Where possible, original accounts by eyewitnesses were drawn on; where these were not available, secondary accounts by reliable authors were employed. No attempt has been made to alter basic events in the cases for the sake of a "better story." Where quoted dialogue appears, it was actually spoken, strongly suggested in primary accounts, or would naturally have taken place in the circumstances.

Here, then, is a representative selection of ghost stories that actually happened to real people in real situations. Because they occurred in different places and at different times around the globe, these strange phenomena have an obvious universality. Furthermore, they are all linked together by the fact that no natural or physical explanations can really account for them.

As a former Lay Fellow of the American Society for Psychical Research, I wish to thank that dedicated organization for the use of its library facilities and publications. In particular, I would like to thank Mrs. Fanny Knipe, executive secretary of the ASPR, for her patience and invaluable assistance.

David C. Knight
Dobbs Ferry, New York
Fall 1983

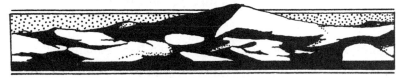

ALGERIA

THE APPARITIONAL LEGIONNAIRES

THIS LONG-FORGOTTEN APPARITION CASE HAS SURVIVED only because a veteran of the French Foreign Legion later wrote it down from memory and mailed it to the great French psychical investigator, Professor Charles Richet. Richet then passed it along to the *Société Psychiques* which published it around 1921. The case is significant because—assuming the Legionnaire's story to be the literal truth—it was one of the rare multiple-witness type in which several persons observe an apparition simultaneously.

The author of the account, Legionnaire René Dupré, wrote that the strange incidents happened during fifteen days in May 1912, at a desert outpost approximately 200

1

miles south of the Legion's Algerian headquarters at Sidi-bel-Abbes. At that time, France's Foreign Legion was carrying out the pacification of Morocco against fierce dissident tribesmen.

A *Zone Soumise*, or Pacified Zone, had been established, but nothing really prevented the roaming Arab dissidents' caravans from doing a thriving business in gun-running and other illegal activities. The Zone could only be held if all the oases to the south were in French hands and blockhouse-style forts set up to control the caravan routes. For this work, Legion columns were regularly sent south against the terrible desert winds, the blistering heat, and the cold rains. A typical relief column would march out on foot with its supplies carried on mules or camels. When it took over its assigned blockhouse and the relieved garrison had disappeared north through the sands, it was completely isolated for months.

The Legionnaires endured much hardship in this desert-garrison life. They were literally cut off from the world. There were no radios, no airplane drops of supplies or mail. The food was foul and the water scarce. All but entombed in horrible monotony, the worst in both officers and men was often brought out. Fights were frequent. There was no diversion and no women. It was only surprising, wrote René Dupré, that the men stayed sane.

The Legionnaires had a word for this dreaded monotony: *caffard*. If an officer or a non-com asked a depressed-looking Legionnaire if he had *caffard* and the man replied yes, the officer understood, for likely as not he had it himself. Thus, the men in these lonely outposts welcomed a patrol outside or even an attack by enemy tribesmen to break the monotony.

Dupré's infantry company, along with two others, arrived

at one of these desert blockhouses late in March 1912. But they had run into trouble on the march south. Arab tribesmen had set an ambush for the Legion column about two miles from their destination. A sharp fire-fight had ensued and, before the tribesmen were finally driven off, five Legionnaires—two from Dupré's company—lay dead. The major in charge of the column had ordered the bodies buried and the graves covered with stones so that animals would not disturb them.

Some two weeks after their arrival at the blockhouse, Dupré was walking guard duty on the parapet. It was past midnight when he saw his commanding officer leave his headquarters and stroll out on the parapet, as was his habit before retiring.

"*Alors*, Dupré," said the officer quietly, "we've only been here a couple of weeks and I think you've got *caffard* already."

"*Oui, mon capitain.* That's so."

"Well, with luck we'll be relieved in three months. Meanwhile, keep a sharp eye out. We don't want these Arabs sneaking up on us."

Dupré saluted and the officer passed on. A half hour went by and Dupré kept scanning the bleak, shadowy desert as he walked his post. A low crescent moon bathed the rolling sands with an eerie yellow glow. Suddenly he saw something move against a dune some four or five hundred yards to the north. Dupré halted and strained his eyes. Then he saw that it was a man walking toward the blockhouse. Dupré automatically raised his rifle to the ready position. The man seemed to stagger as he came closer. When the figure had approached another fifty yards, Dupré saw that it was a Legionnaire in uniform. As the man walked, he zigzagged back and forth, as if he were searching for someone or something. It was at this point that Dupré noticed something very queer about the figure: he could see right through it! Camels' tracks and desert stones were plainly visible through the man's uniform.

This was enough for Dupré, and he shouted for the Corporal of the Guard, who came running at the double. Dupré pointed out to him the staggering, diaphanous figure. The amazed corporal stared for a few seconds and then called for the Officer of the Guard.

"Sir," said the corporal, "there seems to be a Legionnaire out there! But I can see right through him!"

The three men, speechless with fascination, watched as the meandering figure with its somehow pathetic sidling motions came still closer.

"My God," whispered the officer finally. "I can see his face now. It's Leduc!"

"That's impossible, sir," breathed the corporal in a hushed voice. "Leduc's dead. We buried him the day of the ambush."

"Then it's his ghost," whispered the officer, shaking his head in disbelief.

"Look, sir," hissed Dupré, "it's disappearing now!"

As the Legionnaires gaped, the filmy figure seemed to melt away into the murky, yellowish sand. Nothing more of the apparitional Legionnaire Leduc was seen that night.

According to René Dupré's account, news of the ghostly visit of their dead comrade spread rapidly through the garrison. The major ordered the nightly guards doubled. He needn't have bothered, for many of the men joined the nightly vigil. The excitement served as a diversion for the Legionnaires and helped to assuage their *caffard*.

Four nights later the phantom of Leduc reappeared about an hour and a half after midnight. Many Legionnaires witnessed it. Once again the forlorn, searching figure was seen to tramp unsteadily toward the blockhouse, then angle off and fade from view against the desert sands. This same performance was repeated on the next night. Some of the Legionnaires claimed they could see smears of blood on Leduc's ghostly face. (He had received a tribesman's bullet through the temple and had died instantly.)

Then the phantasmal scenario changed. Leduc was seen no more for the next few days. The next spectral event happened three nights later when, once again, René Dupré was walking guard duty on the parapet. He was not alone there. A few other Legionnaires, most smoking pipes, were also peering out on the desert wastes. A few minutes after one o'clock, a couple of men pointed off to the north and whispered excitedly.

"Out there!" one cried. "He's coming!"

Dupré saw it too. Far out against the leaden sand the figure of a Legionnaire could be seen weaving along uncertainly, his visored white *kepi* pulled low over his face. The men in the blockhouse watched spellbound as it progressed forward in searching zigzags. When it came within 150 yards of the fort, it weaved off to its left, and the watchers could see its transparent profile. Dupré did not have to call the Corporal and Officers of the Guard, for they were standing right next to him, staring transfixed at the plodding phantom.

"Look at his face!" somebody shouted. "That's not Leduc. It's Sergeant Schmidt!"

"You mean it's his ghost," said the Officer of the Guard. "Schmidt got it with Leduc and the others. They're buried out there, remember?"

The men of the garrison stared as the figure of Schmidt dissolved against the sandy wastes. It was next seen two nights later in a repeat performance, marching along uncertainly as if looking for something it had lost. It was then that

a small, thoughtful Legionnaire named Renaud made an interesting remark. Everyone listened.

"I think I understand," Renaud said slowly but clearly. "I think they're looking for each other. We all know what great friends they were."

René Dupré's account then details the friendship between the two men. It was a rather unusual one in the Legion. Normally Frenchmen stuck with Frenchmen, Germans with Germans, Poles with Poles, and so on. But the French private and the German sergeant had taken to each other from the first. They went on leave in Oran together, got drunk together, ate together, fought together, marched together. And on Camerone Day—that day each year when the story of the Legion's sacrifice in Mexico is read to all Legionnaires wherever they are—Schmidt and Leduc sat and listened together.

The climax of the case occurred on the fifteenth day after the apparition of Leduc was first seen. Dupré was not on guard that night but he was watching out of curiosity. So were perhaps thirty other Legionnaires, puffing on pipes and gazing out across the dunes to the north.

Around two o'clock in the morning their patience was rewarded. Men began to whisper and point. Far out on the wastes, two figures could be seen striding along together, as if on the march. They did not approach the blockhouse but strode along parallel to it. Their white *kepis* were distinctly those of Legionnaires. The figures were too filmy and far away for anyone in the garrison to see their faces, yet everybody assumed they were Leduc and Schmidt. Dupré wrote that they were seen for perhaps a minute, no more. As they faded out over a dune, the watchers saw that one figure raised its arm, as if in a gesture of farewell. The phantom figures were never seen again.

In his account, René Dupré made no attempt to explain the curious appearances. He merely wrote down what happened. The case was never formally investigated, nor were any of the observers—including Dupré—ever tracked down and questioned. But the case is similar to others in which ghosts of persons who have met violent deaths have remained for a time to haunt the places where they met their ends. The ghosts of some brutally murdered people have been known to linger for a hundred years or more, bound to such places by resentment for the deed done to them. According to those who believe in an afterlife, this seriously impedes their progress in the next world.

But in the case of the slain Legionnaires, their ghosts did not linger long. Perhaps they were drawn to the blockhouse as the destination they never reached. Or maybe they were drawn to their surviving comrades out of the deep devotion to the Legion that all Legionnaires feel. Or perhaps, as Renaud suggested, the two spirit wanderers wished to find each other. Having done so, they decided to march off together—as they had in life—to the next world.

THE GHOSTLY DOUBLE
OF LOUIS RODGERS

PSYCHIC INVESTIGATORS DEFINE A "DOUBLE" AS A GHOSTLY
or apparitional counterpart of the physical body; when dislo-
cated from the living body, the double may temporarily
move about in space and appear to others. The Germans
have their own name for this phenomenon—*Doppelgänger*, or
"double-walker," which is a ghost, or double, of a living
person. Yet another term for this rare phenomenon is *biloca-
tion*, in which a person is seen simultaneously in two places.
One of the most remarkable cases of this type in psychic
history was that of the ghostly double of Louis Rodgers.

It was in the spring of 1937 that the name of Louis
Rodgers burst into the world's headlines. His apparently
incredible ability to appear simultaneously in places

9

hundreds of miles apart baffled the experts at the time. It still does today. Physicians, scientists, researchers into the supernatural, even the police subjected Louis Rodgers to unprecedented scrutiny. They tracked down his every contact, followed him relentlessly, and once even locked him up—and still his double was seen in distant places where Louis was not supposed to be. If Louis was playing a hoax on everyone, it was surely the most skilled in the annals of psychic research.

Louis Rodgers was an Englishman who had come to settle in Australia in 1931. Then thirty years old, he went to Melbourne and set himself up in business as a professional medium—a person through whom communication is made between the living and the dead. He was a good-looking young man, with long black hair and plenty of charm. Women, especially older women clients, liked him. About his lips there played an enigmatic, rather sad smile, and this too had its effect on his female customers. No one seemed to know much about Louis; there was an air of mystery about him, and he cultivated this quality as well. It was not long before he had built up a thriving business. His specialty was bringing back the beloved husbands, children, and other deceased relatives of his clients, usually once a week in afternoon seances. And he performed this service for all at reasonable rates.

As the years advanced, business went well in Rodgers' thickly draped consulting rooms. His appointment book was always full. Word of his skill at summoning the spirits from the world beyond spread rapidly. He was fond of saying, "I am at the mercy of the spirits. Wherever they call me I must go." Many people regarded this as the professional patter of a medium—until one summer day in 1935 when two of Rodgers' clients happened to meet on a street in Melbourne.

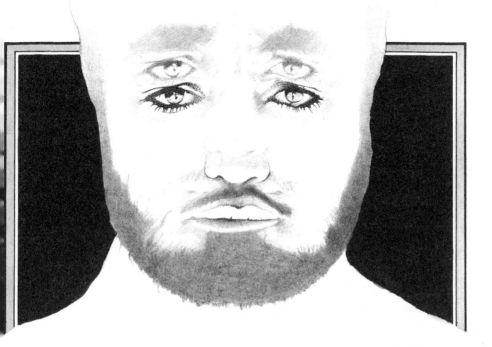

"I didn't know," said one lady, "that Mr. Rodgers had moved to Sydney. But my sister saw him there last Thursday afternoon and had quite a long conversation with him."

"But that's impossible," objected the other woman. "Mr. Rodgers was at *my* house last Thursday afternoon. He brought back my poor dead husband."

From this instance and others like it, the rumors about Louis Rodgers' double started and began to spread. Examples of his "double appearances" grew more numerous. People would be speaking to Louis in one place at a certain time and learn later that someone else had seen and sometimes had even spoken with him in another place many miles away. All this, of course, served to enhance Louis's reputation as a medium and his business boomed. Now he was more than ever the man of mystery and living proof that other dimensions than the worldly one must exist. A few of his clients even dared to ask him about his rumored double appearances. When they did, Louis would merely smile his sadly enigmatic smile and run his fingers through his long black locks. If he replied at all, it was with his favorite phrase: "Wherever the spirits summon me I must go."

At about this time, Dr. Martin Spencer began to read and hear about the man who could be in two places at once. Spencer was Director of Australia's Victoria Institute for Psychic Research and had build up a reputation as an investigator who could ferret out hoaxes and reveal tricksters who attempted to fool psychic investigators. He had heard scores of tales like the Rodgers rumor, and as a professional, he knew that perhaps only one in a hundred of them was worth looking into. Nevertheless, so persistent were the Rodgers' stories that Spencer decided this might be one of those worthy few. He dispatched two scientists from his Institute to ask Rodgers whether he would be willing to undergo some tests of his alleged powers. But Louis angrily refused.

Intrigued by Rodgers' refusal, Dr. Spencer himself went to talk to the medium. He asked Louis why he feared an investigation. After all, he urged persuasively, it would be in the name of science and mankind; if such phenomena existed, more ought to be learned about them. Louis replied that his clients trusted and respected him and he did not want to lose their confidence; besides, he said, he did not want a lot of scientific hypothesizing to endanger his career.

In the end, however, Rodgers reluctantly agreed to participate in a series of experiments. But Spencer and his Institute colleagues were not the only ones who were interested in Louis Rodgers. Australian law enforcement authorities were taking notice of his purported powers. The police, wondering whether the medium was pulling some sort of confidence game, were keeping a close watch on Rodgers and his movements.

In April 1937 Dr. Spencer commenced his experiments with the medium. Spencer had received Louis's promise not to leave Melbourne for three weeks. Rodgers also agreed to allow Spencer's investigators to "tail" him in his comings and goings from home and consulting room. Other investigators were also planted in Sydney, over 400 miles away, and in a few additional places where Louis's alleged double had appeared.

Three days after the experiments began, on April 8, an investigator in Sydney reported to Spencer by phone. He had found out that a man named Louis Rodgers had checked into a downtown hotel. The investigator said that he had gone to the hotel—which he was now phoning from—and knocked on the appropriate door. The door was opened, said the investigator, by a tall good-looking man with long black hair. To the investigator's question, this man had replied that, yes, he was Louis Rodgers, and he had just come from Melbourne. The investigator had then gone immediately to a phone to ring up Dr. Spencer in Melbourne.

"So," said the investigator into the mouthpiece, "he's here."

"No, he's not," replied Spencer. "I'm having lunch with him at this moment."

Dr. Spencer was not much impressed by this. He knew

that two slick operators, looking quite a bit alike, could easily pull off such a stunt. As he went on with his lunch, he told Louis Rodgers as much.

Rodgers replied, with an impatient shake of his head, that he was getting rather weary of the investigation. Then he said, "On April 12, I will prove once and for all I have this extraordinary power. Then perhaps you'll leave me alone."

Accordingly, on April 12, Louis was conducted to Dr. Spencer's own office and locked in. With three other witnesses present, the medium asked Spencer for some kind of password—the first one that entered his mind.

Immediately Dr. Spencer said, "Lilac."

Everyone in the room sat there in silence for about an hour. Suddenly the phone rang. Spencer answered it. It was an investigator in Sydney who said that he had just seen in one of the city's crowded streets a man who looked exactly like Louis Rodgers. Tension mounted in the locked room. Everyone felt it except Rodgers who, evidently bored with the whole thing, simply gazed out of the window.

Then at 5 P.M., an hour after the first call, the telephone rang again. Dr. Spencer fumbled for the receiver and also flipped on a tape recorder to monitor the call.

"This is Sydney," came the operator's voice. "I have a call for you."

In his receiver Spencer heard the unmistakable voice of the medium sitting in the same room with him: "This is Louis Rodgers. The password is 'Lilac'. . ."

Five years later during World War II, Louis Rodgers was killed while serving with the Australian Army in Europe. No official pronouncement was ever made on whether Louis's ghostly double was a real phenomenon or a fraud. But once, in a relaxed moment, Dr. Spencer confided to a friend that he leaned toward the former.

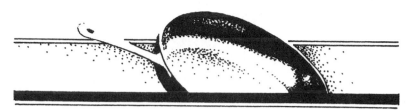

THE SÃO PAULO POLTERGEIST

THE STONE-THROWING—COMMON IN POLTERGEIST activity—that took place in and around São Paulo, Brazil, is among the best witnessed in modern times. Occurrences were observed by a police inspector, a priest, an attorney general, a number of schoolteachers, numerous journalists, and even some physicists. But the poltergeist attack on the household and family of Don Cid de Ulhoa Centro was one of the most savage and disturbing of all. Like the Great Flood of the Bible, it lasted for forty days and forty nights.

The disturbances began on Sunday, April 12, 1959. Don Cid's wife, Dona Regina, and her maid, Francesca, were preparing the noon meal. His three children were playing in

15

the front hallway of his São Paulo hacienda. Don Cid himself was seated in his favorite chair reading a newspaper.

Suddenly there were two sharp thuds. Astonished, Don Cid called to his wife in the kitchen.

"Was that the children? What are they doing?"

"I don't know," Dona Regina called back. "I'm very busy. Can you go and see?"

Don Cid sighed, put down his paper, and strolled out into the hacienda's main hallway. There he discovered his children cowering and almost in tears.

"Father, somebody's throwing stones at us," said one of the children.

Don Cid saw two stones lying on the floor. He bent over and picked them up. "Did you see who it was?" he asked.

"No," said another child, shaking his head. "They just dropped down beside us."

Frowning, Don Cid thought it over. This part of the hallway opened into the courtyard. Someone could have tossed the stones from out there. Maybe some friend or acquaintance was playing a practical joke. Don Cid went out into the courtyard, but he could see nothing amiss. He had been outside for only a couple of minutes when he heard shouts from the hacienda.

Don Cid rushed back inside and discovered more stones and rocks falling in the front hallway, the drawing room, the pantry, and the kitchen. Indeed, they appeared to be dropping all over the interior of the hacienda—except, strangely, in a room where the children had taken refuge.

While his household was terrified and took cover where they could, Don Cid remained calm and kept his head. He was not a man who got rattled easily. With great curiosity—almost with a scientific air—he tried to figure out the trajectories of the dropping stones. He examined the walls and ceilings for holes through which the objects might be coming. He found none. Puzzled, he next went the rounds of the rooms and made sure all the doors and windows were shut and locked.

At this point, the rocks were not only dropping steadily, but they had also begun to ricochet off the walls. Others rolled about on the floors as if they were alive. Still others seemed to be bouncing up into the air like jumping jacks.

Intensely curious about the strange phenomena, Don Cid caught a number of the stones in his hands; they were quite warm to the touch. After he had spent some time running about after the rolling, dropping, bouncing stones, he decided to call in some neighbors to witness the alarming events. Gathering to see the falling stones for themselves, these people could no more explain the odd bombardment than Don Cid could. They simply stood dumbfounded as the missiles continued to rain down on the luckless household. But strangely, nobody actually got hit by the falling stones.

Don Cid put up with the disturbances, which waxed and waned in intensity, for another forty-eight hours. Then, being a sincere Roman Catholic, he summoned a priest, Father Henrique de Morais Matos, to try to exorcise the troublesome spirit. In the meantime, the poltergeist activity had become more varied. While occasional stones and rocks still were in evidence, the eerie force had added to its repertory flying crockery, loose vegetables, pots and pans, and other kitchen utensils. Like Don Cid, the priest was an inquisitive man, not given to panic, and he too became more intrigued than terrified by the disturbances. He carefully watched the trajectories of the missiles and noted their direction and velocity.

Then Father Matos decided to conduct an experiment with the flying objects. Seeing an egg floating through one of Don Cid's rooms, he managed to seize it in his hand. Then he placed it in the refrigerator. Keeping a close eye on the various poltergeist events, he soon spotted an egg smashing against a wall of the butler's pantry. Oddly, it did not break but seemed to flutter gently to the floor. The priest picked it up and noted that it was cool to the touch. Hastening to the refrigerator, he opened it and discovered that the egg he had

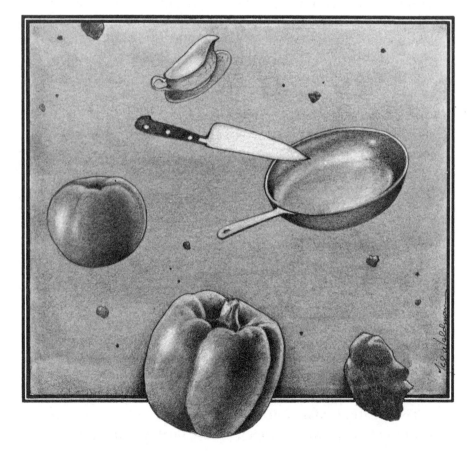

placed on one of the shelves was no longer there. He surmised that somehow the evil force in the house had made it pass through the metal structure of the refrigerator and out into the house.

The priest then thought it time to perform the rites of exorcism. When he had completed this brief service, the disturbances ceased for a time. But the poltergeist was evidently only napping and gathering force for a new attack. About a week and a half later, the activity commenced afresh. Stones once again rained down in Don Cid's hacienda. Even though Father Matos repeated his rites twice more, the poltergeist activity always started up again.

At this stage of the case, suspicion had fallen on the young maid, Francesca, as somehow being the cause of the disturbances. Whenever the events commenced, she seemed to be in or very near the area in question and, in fact, the activity appeared to follow her as she moved from one place to another. Don Cid became convinced of her involvement and kept a sharp watch on the girl's comings and goings. But when he questioned her, Francesca vehemently denied having anything to do with the activity. At length, Don Cid had to admit to himself and others that he had been wrong and that the maid was guilty neither of any trickery nor of causing the events by any natural means.

However, some local spiritualists came forward and claimed that the young maid possessed psychic and mediumistic powers of which she had no knowledge. Mischievous spirits, they said, had been attracted to Francesca's powers and, through her presence, had caused the falling stones and other phenomena. By this time, the São Paulo newspapers had gotten wind of the strange occurrences and had sent reporters to the hacienda. Some of them had been struck by the fact that all through the disturbances, the uneducated girl had remained unconcerned and completely calm. Though some large stones had only narrowly missed her, she had gone on about her kitchen work. When asked why she had no fear, she replied that she "just knew" the objects would never hurt her—and they never did.

Whatever the cause of this remarkable display of poltergeist activity, it ceased after forty days and nights. Relieved, Don Cid and his unnerved family once again took up their normal lives in peace and quiet.

While little is known of the girl Francesca—she left Don Cid's employ shortly after the occurrences—she fits well into the pattern of many poltergeist cases. A girl in her mid-teens, she was doubtless the "focus person" about whom the events centered. In some way, probably without her conscious knowledge, the girl was undergoing mental stress and building up powerful reserves of psychic energy. Finally, according to this theory of psychokinesis, the energy was released and caused the strange physical events.

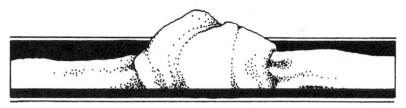

CANADA

THE GHOST
THAT TIED KNOTS

IN 1928 MRS. SIMS' FAMILY MOVED INTO A TWO-STORY HOUSE in one of the French quarters of Montreal. In style the house was also French and had double parlors downstairs, with all of the bedrooms upstairs. Mrs. Sims herself was recently widowed and maintained her own household, but she paid regular visits to her family's house. The family consisted of Mrs. Sims' mother and father, her two older sisters, her five teenaged brothers, and her beautiful young teenaged sister.

At the time of the strange occurrences, the family had lived for about a year in the house. Mrs. Sims had been quite busy and had not found time to visit her family for several weeks. Then one day she got an emotional phone call from one of her older sisters, who informed her that odd things

21

had been happening. Everything in the house that was capable of being tied in a knot *had* been tied in a knot. Mrs. Sims' first reaction was that someone was probably playing a practical joke on the family—maybe one of the teenaged brothers. But she held her tongue. Her sister said that she had not wanted to tell Mrs. Sims of the odd happenings, hoping that they would soon stop. Instead, they had gotten progressively worse.

"Come and see for yourself," urged her sister.

Mrs. Sims did so and found the whole house in a weird state. Just about everything was tied in knots—the drapes hanging across the doorways, the curtains at the windows, and most of the clothing in the closets. Moreover, it was the same kind of knot in every case. Her family then told Mrs. Sims that the knots had first appeared in the back sitting room—one that the teenaged sister was in the habit of using during her leisure time. This girl had taken on the task of looking after her mother's every need, for the older woman's health had not been good.

The members of her family also told Mrs. Sims that the mystifying knot-tying, having begun downstairs, had progressed slowly to the upstairs rooms. In time, it had worked its way into their mother's wardrobe. In fact, the mother's finer pieces of clothing were becoming worn out from the tight twisting knots. And, as soon as family members struggled to untie the knotted garments, new knots appeared in them.

When the phenomenon progressed to one of the brothers' rooms, the boys determined to put the mysterious power to a test. There was a long runner, or cloth, on the young man's dresser that almost surely would be a target for the unseen knot-tier. Before going to bed, the boys placed a number of heavy objects on the runner, among them wrenches from a

tool kit, to see if the ghost could remove them and knot up the fabric. The ghost did just that. In the morning the runner was found in one large bunched-up knot.

After a while it became apparent that the disturbances were centering around the teenaged daughter, Mrs. Sims' youngest sister. They even occurred when the girl was not at home. On one occasion she visited some old friends of the family and left her hat on a table in their hallway. During the visit the girl and the hostess talked about the strange goings-on in the family's house. Later the hostess passed through the hallway and found the teenager's hat turned inside out and the hatband torn off.

The knot-tying phenomena in the Montreal home were to last for six weeks. As the days passed and the knot-tying continued, the members of the family all grew increasingly tense and anxious. On one evening in particular, Mrs. Sims felt that the tension in the air was mounting toward some fresh outbreak of odd happenings. She and her father and mother were the only ones in the house. Sensing that they were all jumpy, Mrs. Sims suggested the three of them go to the dinette in the rear of the house and have a snack. This they did and spent about an hour there eating and chatting. When they emerged from the dinette, they were shocked at what they saw. Like a barricade before them was the largest knot of all!

Standing some three feet high, the knot consisted of some large curtains called portieres, which had hung in the hallway and served as inside doors, and a number of overcoats. The overcoats belonged to Mrs. Sims' five brothers, and they normally hung in a small hall off the dinette. Now they were looped and twisted together with the heavy portières into a giant tangled-up knot. As if the ghost had felt impelled to add a finishing touch to its work, an umbrella which had stood in the front hall rack was jammed upright into the middle of the tangle. Terrified at this eerie sight, Mrs. Sims muttered a hasty good night to her parents and fled from the house.

While this was the largest knot to appear during the six weeks of the disturbances, another big one occurred a couple of days later. On this occasion Mrs. Sims' mother awoke to find the top blanket on her bed twisted up in a single knot in front of her face. After these two events, the frightened parents tried to move out and find somewhere else to live. However, their landlord refused to allow them to do so. They took the landlord to court to force him to break their lease. But the judge deemed there was not enough evidence to grant their request.

Desperate now, the family decided to call on their church for help. Two priests arrived and blessed the house in an effort to exorcise the knot-tying ghost. But this had no effect; it simply continued its work. By this time, news of the strange happenings had gotten into the papers, and people such as spiritualists, detectives, reporters, and others began to come to the house. Many offered to help; others were merely curious.

The disturbed family readily accepted the police's offer of help. The detectives in going through the basement noticed a very bad odor there. None of the family, including Mrs. Sims, had ever smelled it before. The detectives then brought in some bloodhounds, thinking it possible that someone might have been murdered in the house and buried in the basement. One policeman even theorized that the angry spirit of the murdered person might be tying the knots as some kind of warning or sign to the family. But no body was ever found in the basement.

By this time Mrs. Sims' father had grown furious at the antics of the ghost, and he ordered it aloud one night never to touch any of his clothing. So far it had not knotted up any of his garments—not even a necktie. The next morning he found a pair of his best pants turned inside out with a tight knot in each of the legs. He also discovered his hat turned inside out with the band ripped off.

In one of the empty rooms upstairs, the police conducted an experiment to test the powers of the mysterious knot-tier. After locking all the windows in the room tightly, they draped a number of handkerchiefs over the long rod in the closet. Then they locked the door to the room, with one of the detectives retaining the key, and went downstairs to further discuss the strange affair with the family. After waiting about an hour, everyone went back upstairs and the door to the room was unlocked. The family knew what to expect, but the detectives were amazed to see that each handkerchief was tied in a series of tiny knots along its whole length.

The detectives now tried a new idea to find out who was tying the knots. They told each family member to tie knots in some ropes they had brought with them. It turned out that the teenaged girl was the only one to produce the kind of knot used by the ghost. From this the detectives formed the opinion that somehow she had tied the knots "uncon-sciously," and that some "magic spell" had been cast over her by an unseen force or power.

During the final week of the hauntings, it happened that the famous magician and sleight-of-hand artist Blackstone was playing at a theater in Montreal. One evening on stage he mentioned "this house . . . which has such a strange visitor," and he said that he would use his powers to remove the "spell" from the young girl. Presumably Blackstone meant to do this at a distance without visiting the house. Whether the great magician ever did so, Mrs. Sims and the family never found out. Nevertheless, the next day things came to a head.

That evening Mrs. Sims heard her older sister call her mother into the young girl's room. The mother went into the room. The others waited outside and could not hear what was said. Later Mrs. Sims heard her older sister say, "The curtains were blowing wildly and there seemed to be an eerie feeling about the place."

A short time later the mother left the girl's room in stony silence. Observing her, Mrs. Sims thought at the time that she seemed to be afraid to say anything for fear the young girl might hear her. Mrs. Sims and the others never did find out exactly what happened in the room that evening, for neither the mother nor the girl nor the older sister would ever discuss it. In any case, from that day on there was no more mysterious knot-tying, and the relieved and happy family resumed normal lives once again.

THE MOVING COFFINS
OF BARBADOS

AT NIGHT THE MOON SHIMMERS OVER THE SILVER CARIB-
bean and lights up the ornate coral and stone crypt that
stands on a headland of the lovely West Indian island of
Barbados. It is—or was—a family crypt and rests in the
parish churchyard near the sea in the town of Christchurch.
The entrance to the crypt, partially hewn out of the flinty
rock, was once sealed by a massive stone slab.

In times gone by, each time a new coffin was placed inside
the vault, a gang of at least half a dozen strong men was
needed to move the slab aside. In this crypt for a period of
thirteen years, from 1807 to 1820, there occurred periodic
morbid happenings that still defy any natural or scientific
explanation.

The crypt was the property of Colonel Thomas Chase, a well-to-do Englishman who made his home on Barbados. The peaceful island, continually swept by tradewinds, had been occupied by the British as early as 1627. In the minds of many Barbadans, the supernatural occurrences in the crypt were linked with the character of Colonel Chase himself. He was known to be a cruel man with an ungovernable temper, a harsh parent, and a slaveowner who ill-treated his charges.

Having acquired the crypt early in the new century, Chase did not have occasion to use it until July 31, 1807. At that time a Mrs. Goddard, a member of the family, died. When the crypt was opened to receive her heavy lead coffin, it was quite empty. Several months later, in 1808, Mary Anna Chase, the colonel's infant daughter, died of disease. The crypt was opened again, and Mrs. Goddard's coffin was seen in its proper place. Four years passed and then Dorcas Chase, an older daughter of the colonel's, died. On July 6, 1812, when her casket was placed in the crypt, the first two coffins were precisely as they should have been.

A month after Dorcas was entombed, Colonel Chase himself suddenly died. When the gang of workmen removed the slab to place their master's coffin in the crypt, they and members of the Chase family were shocked at what they saw inside. The coffins of Mrs. Goddard, Mary Anna, and Dorcas were discovered in a jumbled state. They had apparently been thrown about like so many sticks of wood. The position of the infant's small casket was the strangest of all. It had been moved or thrown diagonally from the corner where it originally lay to the opposite corner of the tomb.

Before the tomb was resealed with the colonel's body in it, the disturbed coffins were replaced in their proper positions; that is, three on the floor side by side and the other laid on top of them. And this time someone thought to strew the

crypt floor with a thin layer of sand for the purpose of detecting the footprints of possible intruders.

Four years later, in September 1816, another infant family member's body was made ready for burial in the Chase crypt. When the stone slab was pushed aside, the astonished family again found great disorder among the leaden caskets. All four were scattered about as if some crazed giant had been let loose inside the vault. Indeed, it would have taken a giant to do the job, for it took at least four men to lift just one of the adult coffins. It was also discovered that the layer of fine white sand on the crypt floor was undisturbed by footprints or markings of any kind.

Just a few weeks later, the body of another family member, Samuel Brewster, was taken from the parish of St. Phillip and reinterred in the Chase vault. Again the heavy coffins were found scattered about willy-nilly at odd angles. Again, too, there was the fine sand on the floor with no markings to be seen in it. Mystified, the family attending Brewster's interment watched the sweating, grunting workmen as they struggled to replace the coffins in their proper positions: three side by side on the floor and the others laid on top of them. When the gang of men had slid the great stone slab back in place, masons stepped forward to seal up the crypt again with mortar.

After this most recent disturbance of the crypt's coffins, the islanders of Barbados began to mutter and speculate. What or who was perpetrating these ghoulish acts? Various theories went the rounds but none seemed plausible. Had seawater somehow penetrated the crypt and shifted the caskets about? But how could seawater rise through the solid coral and rock to where the churchyard sat one hundred feet above sea level? Volcanic activity could be pretty well ruled out since only the coffins were moved; a force strong enough to do that would certainly have damaged the close-fitting masonry work of the vault. But the blocks were intact and undisturbed.

In addition, the approaches to the crypt were so clearly out in the open that any vandals or pranksters would be easily seen. Even if it were possible for such persons to remove the stone slab and enter the vault, the feat of dislodging the heavy coffins would have required several men, who would have been quickly discovered by the rector, or sexton, of the churchyard. Yet all such speculation seemed silly, for the mortar seal at the entrance had not been broken or tampered with in any way.

Even so, stories of the haunted crypt and its restless dead sent shivers of apprehension through the islanders. While they would not go near the churchyard at night, dozens of Barbadans flocked within gazing distance of the crypt by day. They would point and whisper about the "duppies," as spectres and evil spirits were called on the island.

There were other murky rumors circulating among the populace. It was whispered that Dorcas Chase had slowly starved herself to death because of her father's cruelty toward her. In addition, some believed that Colonel Chase had died by his own hand, perhaps out of remorse for causing his daughter's death; after all, the two had been interred in the crypt within a month of each other. It was also generally assumed by everyone that, since the disturbances had dated from Colonel Chase's burial, he must be unwelcome there, and someone or something had made a violent effort to expel him.

At any rate, in the next few years the energetic Governor of Barbados, Lord Combermere, became increasingly concerned about the alarm these rumors were causing. Combermere determined to seize the first opportunity to investigate the matter and get to the bottom of it. He knew, too, that the Chase family wished to have the affair cleared up officially. His chance came in early July of 1819 when the next death occurred in the family. The body of Thomasina Clarke was placed in its leaden casket and the crypt opened to receive it. Lord Combermere was on hand with officials of his staff when, for the fourth time, the coffins were discovered in great disarray.

Lord Combermere's wife wrote in her journal: "In my husband's presence, every part of the floor was sounded to ascertain that no subterranean passage or entrance was concealed. It was found to be perfectly firm and solid; no crack was even apparent. The walls, when examined, proved to be perfectly secure. No fracture was visible, and the sides, together with the roof and flooring, presented a structure so solid as if formed of entire slabs of stone. The displaced coffins were rearranged, the new tenant of that dreary abode was deposited, and when the mourners retired with the funeral procession, the floor was sanded with fine white sand in the presence of Lord Combermere and the assembled crowd. The door was slid into its wonted position and, with the utmost care, the new mortar was laid on so as to secure it. When the masons had completed their task, the Governor made several impressions in the mixture with his own seal, and many of those attending added various private marks in the wet mortar. . . ."

From that moment on, the whole island seethed with speculation about what the next opening of the now notorious crypt might reveal. The islanders were boiling with excitement, and they found the waiting hard. At length, after the crypt had remained sealed for nine months, Combermere agreed to the vault's being unsealed on April 18, 1820.

It was the big event of the year. Entire towns turned out as if it were a public holiday—which in fact the event had become. Islanders by the hundreds surged toward the brow of the hill above Christchurch to gape in anticipation at the celebrated crypt in the churchyard. There they waited in hushed silence and superstitious awe for the arrival of the Governor.

Excited murmurs whipped through the crowds when at

last Lord Combermere made his appearance. The nobleman first examined the vault, satisfying himself that all was as it had been at the sealing nine months before. The mortar was unbroken, and the impressions of his official seal were etched as sharply as the day they had been made. Each man who had made his private mark also satisfied himself that it was unaltered.

Lord Combermere then commanded the workmen to break the official seal. The masonry yielded as usual to their tools but, when several workmen tried to move the great stone slab, it resisted their efforts. Even when greater force was applied, the stone could not be budged. The onlookers were beside themselves with suspense. Looks of wondering dismay passed from one islander to the next—but only for a short while. As if their combined energy and anticipation gave inspired strength to the workmen's efforts, the slab moved about an inch.

Additional men were ordered to help, and inch by inch the stone was slid aside until there was sufficient space to enter. The Governor and others were dumbfounded when they discovered why the slab had been almost impossible to move. One of the leaden coffins was standing on end, with its other end resting solidly against the stone slab. How this heavy object had come to rest in this remarkable position was a mystery, for the fine sand on the crypt floor bore no footprints nor was it in any way disturbed.

The other coffins were confusedly tossed about the tomb, some with their heads down and others up. The casket of one of the infants had been hurled with such force against one of the crypt walls that a deep dent had been made in the stone where one corner had struck. Another leaden casket had been flung down the steps which led to the bottom of the crypt.

Horrified, the Chase family gave orders for all the caskets to be removed at once from the crypt and buried in graves elsewhere. After this the vault was abandoned and was never again used as a burial place.

While the mysterious Barbados crypt case has been probed by several investigators, no one has yet come up with a satisfactory explanation of the occurrences there. Indeed, some theories seem more preposterous than the events they purport to clarify. Vandalism? Voodooism? The restless spirit of Dorcas Chase avenging itself on her father? Above all, who or what was the powerful and enigmatic force that lifted the heavy leaden coffin and propped it feet-up against the crypt's stone slab?

CHINA

THE FORTUNE COOKIE
POLTERGEIST

IN THE TEEMING BRITISH CROWN COLONY OF HONG KONG shortly before World War II, there occurred a case of poltergeist activity with a very unusual aspect. The locale was a popular Chinese restaurant called The Dragon's Claw. It was one of hundreds in the busy pre-war metropolis but, like many others, it did not survive the long Japanese occupation of the 1940s.

The owner of The Dragon's Claw was a man in his early sixties named Ah Fong. Ah Fong had done well with his restaurant for several years. His location was a good one in the center of the city and he made sure that the ingredients in his dishes were of the best quality. In addition, he paid his cooks well and consequently he had his pick of the finest ones to be had. Because of his insistence on culinary excellence, Ah Fong attracted a good clientele in Hong Kong.

Among his customers, he served many British officers stationed in the colony and also American and European businessmen who frequently visited the city and nearby Kowloon. Unlike many Hong Kong restaurateurs, Ah Fong had learned of the popularity in American Chinese establishments of fortune cookies containing cheery or prophetic messages. So he had instituted the practice at The Dragon's Claw. Not only did foreigners enjoy reading and laughing over the sentiments on the little slips of paper, but so did his native Chinese clientele.

In the summer of 1937, Ah Fong expanded his restaurant by purchasing an old building in the rear of the property. With the increase in the number of tables, he had to hire a few more waiters to serve them. One of these was a fifteen-year-old lad named Chin-luck who, dissatisfied with his life as a rural laborer in Central China, had come to Hong Kong to find work. Chin-luck had told Ah Fong that he wanted to become a cook, the finest in China if he could, and begged to be assigned as a kitchen apprentice. Ah Fong said that his kitchen staff was full; perhaps if a vacancy occurred in the future, he would give Chin-luck a chance. So, disappointed but still glad to have a job, Chin-luck went to work as a waiter at The Dragon's Claw. His employer advised him to learn some English as soon as he could, for he would be serving many British and American customers. Chin-luck nodded and said that he would.

And he did. Ah Fong kept a rather fatherly eye on him. He observed that young Chin-luck was soon able to converse effectively with the British army and naval officers who dropped into the restaurant, and that he could also understand and fill the orders of the drawling American businessmen. Yet at times Ah Fong detected a look of discontent—even resentment—on the young waiter's face. The foreigners were always crisply and elegantly dressed, had plenty of money to spend, and sometimes treated the Chinese waiters as inferiors. All this Ah Fong saw and understood, for he had once been a waiter himself.

The disturbances began after Chin-luck had been on the job for six months. One evening in the serving area where the steaming food was assembled for individual guests, a metal cover from a dish of fried rice was seen to rise in the air. It sailed along for about six feet, then dropped to the carpet beside a customer's table. Nobody saw this event except a couple of mystified waiters, one of whom was Chin-luck. The metal top was retrieved and nothing else happened on this occasion. Three nights later a stack of crockery in the kitchen toppled over for no reason that anyone could see and smashed on the floor. About a week later, near midnight when the last customer had left, four waiters and Ah Fong himself saw a bundle of new chopsticks take off from a serving table and fly for some fifteen feet out into the dining area. They dropped with a loud cracking noise just short of the bar.

The waiters, including Chin-luck, began to chatter about the strange events. They asked Ah Fong what it all meant. Ah Fong, who was an avid reader, shrugged and shook his head. He had, he said, read of such things but he had never seen them before. He told his employees not to worry, to carry on with their work; if anyone saw anything else of an odd nature, he should report it to him immediately.

Up to this point none of the poltergeist activity had affected, or been noticed by, the guests. But in the next weeks this was to change. In the first such event, Chin-luck was carrying an uncovered dish of shrimp and beansprouts to a table occupied by a British major and his wife. When he was still three or four feet away from their table, Ah Fong and a waiter beside him saw the dish leap off Chin-luck's tray, overturn on the major's arm, and drop to the floor. Surprised and then furious, the major leaped up, brushing the food from his uniform and calling Chin-luck a "clumsy oaf." Ah Fong rushed over with a napkin and helped clean the major up, apologizing profusely for the unfortunate accident. Chin-luck also assisted and said several times he was sorry. Finally the major calmed down and the incident was soon forgotten by the couple. Later Chin-luck, when questioned by his employer, denied any knowledge of why the dish had flown off the tray as it had.

Fresh incidents now began to occur in the presence of guests—at least one every two or three days. Once a bottle of soy sauce elevated itself from the table of three astonished patrons and spilled all over the tablecloth. Chin-luck, whose table it was, came quickly with a cloth and cleaned it up. Another time, as he was picking up a cocktail from the bar, he and the bartender were amazed to see a wine bottle leave its rack above them and crash to the floor. One night the top to a metal tureen of shark's fin soup became airborne, sailed five or six feet through the air, and struck a patron's leg. Chin-luck apologized and retrieved the tureen top, for it occurred at his table.

Then began the poltergeist activity involving the fortune cookies, which lasted just one week. The cookies were made on the premises of The Dragon's Claw by one of the cooks who doubled as a baker. Suddenly, at the beginning of this week, several of the patrons began complaining to their waiters about the way the cookies tasted. Some guests, when biting into them, discovered they contained blobs of hot Chinese mustard; others complained theirs were filled with black pepper. This, Ah Fong noted, happened most frequently at the tables in Chin-luck's station, although other waiters were getting the same complaints.

After two days of this, Ah Fong summoned the baker and

asked him frankly whether he had been stuffing the fortune cookies with the condiments. The man denied it vigorously. He had been making his batches as usual, cutting up the dough, then twisting the pieces up into individual cookies before sliding them into the oven. True, he sometimes left a batch unattended before doing the twisting process, and somebody could have tampered with it. But he doubted it. At any rate, this ended the first phase of the fortune cookie incidents.

During the middle of the week, the fortune cookies took to the air. In the kitchen, cookies in groups of three or four were seen to rise from their cookie tins and fly for several feet through the air before dropping to the floor. Out in the dining room, particularly at Chin-luck's station, baskets of the fortune cookies left waiters' trays, flew for short distances, and tumbled to the floor. Other cookies rose individually or in pairs from patrons' tables, became briefly airborne, and scattered to the carpet. Ah Fong was standing in the vestibule one evening surveying his clientele when he saw three fortune cookies sail toward him menacingly and then drop noiselessly at his feet.

By Friday of that final week, Ah Fong was worried. Although the flights of the fortune cookies had apparently ended and all was momentarily in order, customers were beginning to ask him what was wrong at The Dragon's Claw. Was the place haunted or jinxed or what? Some of his oldest Oriental patrons were suggesting that ancestral gods might be displeased for some reason. Furthermore, business was starting to fall off noticeably.

The climax of the fortune cookie affair came during the evening meals on Sunday. Actually nothing of a spectacular nature occurred to alarm the diners as they enjoyed the restaurant's fine cuisine. But around nine thirty Ah Fong, who was keeping an eagle eye on his patrons, saw a British rear-admiral rise from his table and walk toward him. He was shaking his head. The admiral showed him a slip of paper he had found in one of his fortune cookies. On it was crudely scrawled in English, "british get out of china." It was written in pencil, and all the letters were lower case. The

admiral was nice about the slur and even joked about it. Ah Fong expressed his regret and said he would investigate. He took the matter seriously. The last thing he wanted—especially for his business—was to stir up resentment between the British and the Chinese. Ah Fong also noted that the admiral's table was in Chin-luck's station.

First Ah Fong called the baker to his office. He showed the man the slip of paper and asked if he knew how it could have gotten into the fortune cookie. The baker said he had no idea. Besides, he pointed out, the slips he put in the cookies were printed ones, not handwritten. He kept a basket of them handy and inserted one as he twisted up each cookie. He never read them; he hardly looked at them as he performed this operation. He supposed anyone could have put the offending slip in his basket. Satisfied, Ah Fong dismissed the baker.

Next, Ah Fong obtained samples of each waiter's handwriting. This was readily available from the food orders they took. He compared each man's handwriting with the crude writing on the slip in the admiral's fortune cookie. He paid particular attention to Chin-luck's handwriting. But he could find no satisfactory evidence. All of the waiters wrote in rather crude English, frequently leaving out capital letters.

Now Ah Fong knew little or nothing about psychical investigation—indeed, that science was still in its infancy—but he wasn't blind, either. From all that he had seen in the past weeks, it was obvious that somehow the presence of Chin-luck had something to do with the disturbances at The Dragon's Claw. He did not want to dismiss the boy out of hand for he had become fond of him. He decided to try an experiment. Summoning Chin-luck, he said candidly that he was very worried about the recent odd happenings; they were bad for business, he said, and he suspected that in some way that no one understood, Chin-luck was at the root of them. There was nothing dishonorable in this, he said kindly. Perhaps, he told the boy, something was bothering him that he was not consciously aware of. Who could understand such things?

So Ah Fong told the boy that he wished him to return home for two months. He had been working very hard and a vacation would do him good. He would, he added, keep him on half-pay during his absence. When he returned, Ah Fong promised, a place would be found for him as a cook's apprentice. Chin-luck was overjoyed and left the next day. With his departure, the disturbances ceased altogether. When Chin-luck returned and happily started his new job in the kitchen, they did not recommence.

This case of poltergeist activity centering around the teenaged Chin-luck is not so much remarkable for the flying objects involved. As in similar cases the boy, evidently upset in some way, had bottled up a great deal of psychokinetic (PK) energy which, when subconsciously released, manifested these events. It may even have accounted somehow for the condiments finding their way into the fortune cookies when the baker's back was turned. The unusual aspect of the case lies in the mystery of how such energy could have produced the writing, however crude, on the slip of paper found in the fortune cookie.

THE HUNCHBACKED
GHOST GIRL OF BRISTOL

IN THE EARLY 1900S, THE WIDOW OF A BRITISH ARMY COL-
onel and her three daughters came to live in an elegant house
in Bristol. The widow, Mrs. Marsh, had taken a long lease on
the house, for the rent was not as much as she had expected.
The reason for this she learned only later: the house, which
was situated on Upper Belgrave Road, was reputed to be
haunted. Even so, Mrs. Marsh reminded herself, haunted or
not, the residence was a fine bargain and she and her children settled in with the intention of staying for some time.

From neighbors and other local people, Mrs. Marsh came
to find out something about her alleged resident ghost. It
was supposed to be the specter of a servant girl who had once
lived and worked in the house. Described as "horrible and

palefaced," she was said to have been the illegitimate daughter of a rich man who had owned the house a half century earlier. One old woman who remembered her commented, "The unfortunate creature could not have been uglier." Besides being half-witted, the servant girl had been hunchbacked, snaggletoothed, and very sallow-faced. "She always wore a cheap pink dress," the old woman recalled. "The poor thing lived a miserable life, often beaten by her father and half-starved. In the end, you know, she drowned herself in that pool in your garden."

After Mrs. Marsh and her daughters had been in the house for a few weeks, the widow found that she had a problem. She was unable to hire a housemaid who would live in. Mrs. Marsh rightly suspected that the reputed ghost was keeping servants away. But as yet, neither she nor her daughters had seen anything of the humpbacked ghost girl.

One day, however, as one of the daughters started to go up the stairs, she passed a young girl who was wearing a pink dress. As busy as if her life depended on it, she was vigorously sweeping the stairs with a brush and pan. The widow's daughter, assuming that her mother had hired a temporary maid, hardly gave the sweeping girl a glance. But, as she said later, that half-glance had left her with a distinct feeling of repugnance.

"You should have seen her, Mother," commented the daughter. "She was terribly untidy—even slovenly. Her cap was soiled and all askew on her head, and she looked decidedly humpbacked. And her face! It was so white and unhealthy looking."

"It would seem," said Mrs. Marsh wryly, "that that was probably our ghost girl."

The next time, the ghost girl was seen by another of the widow's daughters. She, too, met the apparition on the stairs. The ghost girl was clad in the same pink dress, but this time she seemed aware of the daughter's presence. She grinned hideously as she slithered past the daughter and was still doing so over her shoulder as she closed a door behind herself.

Exactly one week later, the widow's third daughter had an encounter with the ghost girl. All alone in the house at the time, this daughter went down into the basement to get some hot water. Returning upstairs, she was dumbfounded when she opened the kitchen to find the hunchbacked figure of the girl in the pink dress. The figure appeared to be busy doing something at the kitchen range, with her back toward the daughter.

"Why-why," stammered the daughter, "what on earth are you doing here?"

The deformed ghost girl whirled around, an impertinent leer on her sallow face. Then, without uttering a word, she scuttled off into an adjoining room. There was no other exit from this room, as the daughter well knew.

"And now," muttered the girl, who was a young woman of some spirit, "I'm going to catch you face to face!"

But when the daughter entered the room, which was the scullery, she found it empty. Of the deformed ghost girl in the pink dress there was no sign whatsoever. Suddenly very frightened, the daughter turned and ran up the stairs. On the first landing, she paused a moment to catch her breath. She was horrified to see, grinning at her through the window of the landing, the white pallid face of the ghostly housemaid she had seen only a minute ago in the kitchen. Moreover, the landing window happened to be thirty feet above the ground!

"How I ever got out of that house," she said later, "I'll never know. But I did."

In fact, she was found by her mother on the porch of the house in a dead faint. So sick did she become afterward that she was sent to the seashore at Brighton to recover. This took several months. In the meantime, Mrs. Marsh determined to look for another house—one that she and her daughters would not have to share with a ghost.

But the ghost girl was seen once more before they moved out. On this occasion, Mrs. Marsh and one of her daughters were having afternoon tea in the parlor. With them was the vicar of a nearby church, Mr. Bates-Tucker, who had recently been transferred to Bristol. Neither of the women had mentioned the ghost to Reverend Bates-Tucker, and being new in the neighborhood, he presumably knew nothing of it. The clergyman was just about to sip his second cup of tea when the women saw him set his cup down and stare with astonishment toward the kitchen door.

"I say," began Mr. Bates-Tucker, "who is that odd-looking person? I thought you ladies lived alone here."

The women looked in the direction Bates-Tucker was pointing. There, in the act of passing from the hallway through the open kitchen door, they saw the pink-clad figure of the ghost girl. Just before the apparition disappeared into the kitchen, it swung its head about and leered at the three onlookers. A few seconds later, the ladies and the clergyman searched the kitchen but found no one there. Mrs. Marsh was quite shaken, for it was the first time she had seen the ghost with her own eyes. The women then explained to Reverend Bates-Tucker the trouble they had been having, and how they were determined to move out of the haunted house.

About three years after the Marshes vacated the house on Upper Belgrave Road, an English psychic investigator and noted ghost-hunter paid it a visit. He subsequently reported that, near the front door, he caught sight of a dishevelled and repulsive-looking little maidservant in a dirty pink dress. The apparition grinned at him, then slipped away through a door at the rear of the hall.

This researcher further reported that the family who moved into the house after the Marshes left remained less than a month. The tenants after that stayed an even shorter time. Thereafter, the house stood empty, and as the investigator was fond of saying, he was sure it would stay that way—except for the apparition in the pink dress.

THE HAMMERING FIST
OF CALVADOS CHATEAU

JUST ABOUT EVERYONE IN THE AREA KNEW THAT THE OLD Norman chateau had been the scene of queer phenomena and the haunting place of malicious ghosts. But when the new owners, the de X. family, inherited the small chateau in 1867 and took up residence in it, they had little inkling of just how violent the disturbances were to become.

In October, just after the family had moved in, the phenomena began—nocturnal noises, blows, rappings, and other queer sounds. Then they abruptly ceased for more than seven years, only to recommence in the year 1875.

These ghostly events were well attested to by numerous witnesses. Chief among them was the chateau's owner himself, Monsieur de X., who later agreed to let his journal of the disturbances be published in the *Annals of Psychic Science* for 1893, provided his family's names were not revealed. "The honesty and intelligence of the owner of this chateau," wrote the *Annals'* editor, "cannot be questioned. . . . He himself noted down every day all the extraordinary facts which he and the inhabitants of the chateau witnessed, just as they occurred."

When the new disturbances broke out on October 12, 1875, fresh snow stood all around the chateau; yet no footprints were discovered in it anywhere about the grounds. Monsieur de X. secretly rigged threads across the doorways and other openings to the building, but he never found them broken.

At first Monsieur de X. refused to believe that the strange noises in the chateau were of supernatural origin. He thought they could very well be the work of living people who, if they could manage to frighten his family sufficiently, would force him to sell the chateau for a song. He therefore conducted a painstaking search of the whole structure from top to bottom. He sounded the walls and the cellars for long-forgotten passageways by which someone might enter. But search as he would, he could find no explanation for the odd noises that now began to intensify.

Next Monsieur de X. purchased two huge watchdogs that were released every night to patrol the grounds. One day the animals set up such a loud barking around a thicket that Monsieur de X. was sure his enemies were hiding within it. He and several of his servants surrounded the tiny woods and released the dogs. The animals rushed into the woods, but almost immediately their barks turned to plaintive whines, as if they were being scolded by an invisible master. They soon emerged from the thicket with their tails between their legs. Although the thicket was thoroughly searched, no one at all was found there.

Living at this time in the chateau was a Catholic priest, Father Y., who was employed as a tutor to the owner's son. During the next months, most of the disturbances took place in the priest's room. The first thing Father Y. noticed amiss was that his armchair had switched places one evening. He reported this to the owner and his wife, who then accompanied him to his chamber. A thorough search revealed nothing out of the ordinary. Monsieur de X. then hit on the idea of attaching pieces of gummed paper to the armchair, fixing it to the floor. He and his wife then returned to their own quarters, telling Father Y. to call if anything happened.

About ten o'clock that night, the priest heard a series of raps that, while faint, were still loud enough so that the maid, Amalina, heard them in the next room. Next the priest heard a noise like the winding of a large clock in the corner of the room, followed by the grating sound of a candlestick being moved along the mantelpiece. Finally, the frightened priest was sure he saw his armchair start to move.

Not daring to get out of bed, Father Y. reached for his bell rope and gave it a yank. A few minutes later, Monsieur de X. entered the room, tried to calm the clergyman, and began checking the objects in the chamber. He found that the armchair had indeed moved back about a yard—the gummed paper had been torn—and it was also facing in a different direction. A statuette near the mirror had advanced some nine inches. The candlesticks had been shifted. About twenty minutes later, after the owner had once again gone to bed, the priest heard two vicious blows strike resoundingly on the door of his wardrobe.

Whatever was causing the disturbances in the chateau soon developed new techniques. Pieces of furniture were heard being lugged about on upper floors, then dropped with devastating thuds. The owners were amazed to hear footsteps in upper rooms and even spoken conversations resembling their own. Amalina once swore she heard her master's and mistress's voices when both were in a far part of the chateau. The savage, hammering blows continued for many days, but although many tours of inspection were conducted, they turned up nothing.

As the days passed, Monsieur de X. was forced to face the fact that he was up against something decidedly supernatural. He invited friends and clergymen to witness the strange events occurring in the chateau. These people would come, spend a night or two, and often leave in haste, for the hammering blows grew unbearably loud and strident. One night everyone was awakened by the sound of a large ball bouncing downstairs, one step after another. Heavy running noises were heard in the upper corridors. On another night someone was heard dashing up the stairs with apparently superhuman speed. After this event, the whole chateau was shaken with a violent blow, as if a big log or an anvil had been flung to the floor. No one in the great feudal house could pinpoint where these blows came from—nor could anyone sleep on that night.

Four days later, there was a repeat performance: the bouncing ball, the sickening blows shaking the walls nearly to pieces, the rushing footsteps. And there was something new—the quick padding about of an animal. The following night Auguste, the gardener, summoned his master to listen to a long series of taps where he slept. He and Monsieur de X. made thorough inspections of that part of the chateau but found nothing. After they left, the noises began again. The next night "some being" was heard to rush at top speed up the main staircase to the first floor—the sounds of these treads had nothing human about them. Everybody in the chateau heard them; it was as if two legs deprived of their feet were stalking about on their stumps.

The hideous noises continued to rock the feudal structure. By mid-November, galloping sounds began to be heard on the stairs, together with heavy thuddings, as if someone were beating on the chateau's doors. Once a series of forty raps was heard, lasting nearly three minutes. On one particularly bad night with a storm howling outside, a long drawn-out trumpet call was heard, even above the storm. A short while later, nearly everyone heard two ghastly shrieks, as if a woman in agony were pleading for help. Two nights after that, more plaintive cries were heard coming from the main hall, followed by stifled moans from the cellar. Then, after midnight, everyone could hear the pitiful sobs of a woman undergoing some horrible suffering.

Even though Father Y. always locked his room and kept the key with him, he would return to find closed windows open again and furniture moved into odd positions. One time his bed was found on its side with a table pushed under it; another time the table was on top of the bed. Once the priest heard a broom apparently sweeping all by itself outside his room; when Monsieur de X. investigated, the broom was not in its proper place. The owner then attempted to solve the priest's open-window problem by nailing the frame shut; later it was found to be open again, with the nails torn out and no trace of any tool that could have been used. In addition, the priest soon became accustomed to finding his shoes, lamp, and water bottle perched in ridiculous positions when he entered his room.

Two days after Christmas, 1875, Monsieur de X. entered Father Y.'s room and found most of his books—at least one hundred of them—strewn all over the floor. On top of a pile of devotional books was a broom. Only three volumes remained on the shelves—books of the Holy Scriptures.

Meanwhile, the nightly hammering, galloping, knocking, thudding, and other unearthly sounds continued to thunder through the chateau. There seemed to be no relief from them. One day both Father Y. and Madame de X. heard a noise in the priest's chamber. Going to investigate, Madame de X. put out her hand to open the door latch when suddenly the key turned all by itself in the lock, detached itself, and hit her other hand a sharp blow.

Of the violent hammerings on their doors at night, Monsieur de X. wrote in his diary: "To acquire some idea of their violence, one must imagine a wall collapsing, or a horse or cannon balls being thrown against a door. It would be no exaggeration. . . ."

Simultaneously, prolonged walking and running could be heard on upstairs floors—strange steps that were often quite unlike human ones. "No animal," wrote the master of the chateau, "could walk like that; it was more like a stick jumping on one of its ends." These eerie sounds were heard by everyone—master, mistress, guests, and servants alike.

Subsequent psychic investigators who later learned of this famous case often wondered how the de X. household endured these nerve-shattering disturbances for so long. Yet they did. Day after day through the month of January, Monsieur de X.'s diary bristles with meticulous accounts of how many blows were struck, when precisely they occurred, and exactly how many minutes they lasted.

Soon the ghostly presence started to mock everyone in the morning when they came downstairs for breakfast. Every footstep the person took would be matched with a rap until he or she reached the ground floor; if the person stopped, the raps would also stop. Once a clergyman was asked to stay at the chateau for the purpose of exorcising the troublesome spirit. All during his visit, which lasted several days, the ghostly presence remained respectful and quiet. But the day this churchman left, there broke out a whole new set of phenomena more boisterous than before.

Prolonged stampeding noises were heard nearly every night in the upstairs rooms. The rolling, bouncing balls continued their mysterious progress down the stairs and through the corridors—never seen but clearly heard. Dull knocks, rhythmic rappings, shrill cries, weird drummings, frantic running noises, dragging footsteps—all continued to make life miserable for those living in the mansion. Deafening bellows and furious shouts added to the nightly din.

Occasionally the entire chateau would be shaken by terrible blows delivered by what sounded like superhuman fists on the heavy outside doors. Sometimes they came with such machinegunlike rapidity that it was impossible for the meticulous Monsieur de X. to count them. Yet nothing—and no one—was ever seen by anyone.

Then on one beautiful day, Father Y. was reading in his chamber when suddenly a cascade of water poured down the chimney onto his fire, extinguishing it and scattering ashes all about the room. The unfortunate priest's face was covered with soot and he was temporarily blinded.

Three days later, on January 28, 1876, everybody heard the voice of a man in one of the back corridors. Twice it cried, "Ha, ha!" Immediately afterward were struck exactly ten resounding reports that rocked the whole mansion. Then there were choking, coughing noises. A search revealed a broken earthenware plate in front of Madame de X.'s door. It was broken in exactly ten places. No one had ever seen it in the chateau before.

That same night another priest, who had been summoned a few days previously, conducted more rites of exorcism. He also had arranged to have a novena mass said at the holy shrine of Lourdes to supplement his own efforts to "lay the ghost." This priest's rites reached their climax about the time the coughing noises were heard. The latter may conceivably have represented the ghost's "death rattle," for Monsieur de X.'s diary reads: "The Reverend Father had completed his exorcisms and everything has stopped."

But had it? True, a great calm set in over the chateau for a time, but the owner's joy in it was shortlived. More was yet to come. Three days later, Madame de X. was writing at her desk when suddenly an immense collection of medals and crosses clattered down in front of her. Part of the exorcism rites, these holy trinkets had been placed on all the doors of the chateau in an effort to ward off the troublesome spirit. Yet, until then, they had all mysteriously disappeared from the doors the day after they had been placed on them!

Mercifully, all remained peaceful that winter and spring and into the summer. Then toward the end of August, muffled knockings and other noises began to be heard again. Unusually loud knocks were heard in the linen room. One night in September a great shuffling noise was heard in the main drawing room, which at that time was locked. When the owner unlocked the room and entered it, he found the couch and armchairs had all been moved from their usual locations. Now they were arranged as if for a council meeting, horseshoe fashion, with the couch in the middle. As one eyewitness later wrote: "The Devil had had his council. . . ."

A little while later Monsieur de X., probably to compose himself, played for a long while on his small organ. When he had finished and closed up the instrument, some of the melodies he had been playing were repeated note for note in the room for a considerable time.

Some months earlier, the terrified Father Y. had left the chateau, and the owner had engaged another tutor for his son. This new clergyman was not to escape a bit of mischief from the ghost. While Monsieur de X. was away on a trip, the priest heard the organ playing tunes all by itself. When the owner returned, the priest reported this odd occurrence to him. "But," protested Monsieur de X., "I have the key to the organ here in my pocket!" It was true—the instrument had been locked for three days.

Even though the Calvados phenomena grew progressively weaker, Monsieur de X. by this time had had enough of the "diabolical spirit." He sold his bedeviled chateau and went to live elsewhere—this time in peace. But the Calvados chateau case lives on in the annals of ghostdom as one of the most remarkable hauntings ever documented by persons of unquestioned integrity.

The most intense period of the poltergeist activity began on October 12, 1875, and lasted until January 30, 1876, after which it tapered off and finally ceased. Well over 100 separate events were recorded during this period—a high number for a case of just about three and a half months duration. Furthermore, they occurred with almost regular frequency, either on successive days or with only a few days' break between occurrences.

THE POLTERGEIST
THAT TELEPHONED

DURING THE SUMMER MONTHS OF 1967, A GERMAN ATTOR-
ney named Sigmund Adam was completely baffled by
strange goings-on in his law offices in Rosenheim, just south
of Munich. Adam had four telephones in his place of business, but usually only one or two of them were in use at the
same time. The remaining two he had had installed just in
case more calls came in when his workload became heavier
than normal.

When the abnormal telephone activity began, all four
phones would sometimes jangle simultaneously. Secretaries
and lawyers called in for consultation went crazy trying to
answer all the calls. Often the calls got cut off in the middle
of conversations. Furthermore, the phone bills Adam received were obviously far too high for the number of calls
that had actually been placed from his law offices.

Other mysterious irregularities also began to occur. Although there seemed to be no overload on the electrical current, fuses would suddenly blow. Light bulbs overheated and burned out. Large fluorescent fixtures recessed in the ceilings winked out as if a hidden hand had unscrewed them by a fraction of a turn. Excess amounts of developing fluid were discovered to have been poured into the photocopying equipment.

Speculating that there might be irregularities in the electrical supply delivered to his offices, Herr Adam got in touch with both the telephone company and the maintenance department of the Rosenheim power station. Technicians were called in to investigate the strange calls and the electric power disturbances. A sophisticated voltmeter was hooked up to monitor variations in the power supply, and a telephone counter was installed to automatically tabulate the exact time of outgoing calls as well as to record the number and duration of incoming calls.

For the next several weeks, the telephone counter recorded repeated calls to the number 0119. This was the phone company's number giving the correct time of day. Moreover, the automatic counting mechanism revealed that these outgoing calls were made as frequently as five or six times a minute. Yet everyone in the office denied dialing this number. On the voltmeter recorder, a number of big power surges were registered that no one could account for. But Herr Adam and others noticed that these surges often coincided with times when unusual phenomena were happening in the law offices.

By early winter the strange case began to receive publicity in the German press. Both the West German and Bavarian television networks decided to try to document what was going on, and soon their cameras were set up in the Rosen-

heim law offices. Not only did the cameras record the instal-
lation of the electrical monitoring apparatus, but they also
filmed interviews with Herr Adam, his employees, and a
number of the technicians. One of the latter insisted that the
automatic counter had not been lying—the repeated calls to
the number 0119 must have been made from the law offices.
Nevertheless, Herr Adam's employees denied making any
such calls. Subsequently, these documentaries were widely
televised throughout Germany.

Ultimately, the publicity roused the interest of the emi-
nent psychologist and psychic investigator Dr. Hans Bender
of the University of Freiburg. Bender was also chief of the
Institute for Border Areas that had already investigated
some thirty similar cases of paranormal activity. Early in
December the Institute commenced its own probe of the

Rosenheim occurrences. Also requested to participate in the investigation was the well-known Max Planck Institute for Plasmaphysics in Munich. Two physicists from this institute came to check out the voltmeter recorder information and any normal physical phenomena that might have caused the strange events.

Bender and his associates from Freiburg quickly established some fundamental observations. First, the phenomena took place only during office hours. These phenomena— the mysterious phone calls that nobody seemed to be making, the fuses and light bulbs burning out for no apparent reason—were of a kind known to parapsychologists as *psychokinesis,* or PK for short. (PK is the direct influence exerted over a physical system by a person without any known intermediate physical energy or instrumentation; popularly, it is known as "mind over matter.")

Second, it did not take the Bender team long to establish that the PK or poltergeist activity was centering about one of Herr Adam's employees, a nineteen-year-old girl named Annemarie Schaberl. Indeed, the paranormal events usually started when Annemarie arrived at the law offices. When the girl came through the entryway, the lamps hanging above her from the ceiling often started swinging. So regularly did this occur that the Bender team was able to photograph the lights in motion. The team also noticed that the odd events usually happened close to where Annemarie was working or standing; they were less frequent at a distance from her. What was more, when a light bulb exploded, regardless of where it was located, the glass shards always flew *toward* Annemarie.

When the investigators had made a thorough examination of the voltmeter-recorder data, they concluded that the power surges were typical of irregular short-duration forces. Yet the phenomena were highly complex and not really like pure electrical behavior. Moreover, there appeared to be something in their recurring patterns that suggested intelligence and evasiveness.

As the poltergeist events continued, the workers in the law offices became rather accustomed to them. Sometimes they would joke about what odd thing would occur next. Annemarie herself could often foretell when something was about to happen. Once she cried out, "Oh, I have a feeling that the light bulb in the next room is going to explode!" In a couple of minutes it did.

Concerned as he was, Herr Adam could see the humor in the whole situation. "The next thing you know," he joked to Annemarie, "the pictures on the walls will start turning around." This was on a Friday afternoon. On entering the office next Monday morning, Herr Adam saw some large oil paintings begin to rotate on their wall hangings. Bender's team of investigators were able to photograph one of them as it swung through nearly half a circle.

Meanwhile, the strange PK events multiplied. A heavy filing cabinet weighing several hundred pounds twice shifted itself out about a foot from the wall. That Annemarie could have accomplished this seemed scarcely possible for she herself weighed only about 100 pounds. Legal briefs and other documents were mysteriously moved from one location to another without anyone having handled them. Desk drawers slid open all by themselves. One day as Annemarie stood under a heavy chandelier, the fixture began to swing so violently that it dented the ceiling.

As the events continued, the strain began to tell on the girl. She complained of strange spasms in her legs and arms. Herr Adam sent her on a leave of absence, and while she was gone the poltergeist activity ceased completely. In time, Annemarie took a job in another office in town.

Dr. Bender, however, was still much interested in the case. As with so many instances of poltergeist activity, the events had centered about a teenager. In interviewing Annemarie, he learned that she was unhappy and frustrated in her job. The work was tedious and boring, and each day she could hardly wait until it was time to go home. Significantly enough, the equipment that had tabulated the calls to 0119 revealed that they had been counted most frequently toward closing time at Annemarie's office. There was never any proof that she or any of the other employees had dialed that number or had perpetrated any of the other events as a joke. But apparently Annemarie's frustration and restlessness on the job had somehow released sufficient psychokinetic energy to activate the weird events in Herr Adam's law offices—the place where she had felt most discontented.

Subsequently, the young woman cooperated in laboratory tests in PK and ESP at the Institute for Border Areas in Freiburg. Oddly, she was unsuccessful in demonstrating PK ability, even when tested with the same kind of voltmeter recorder that had been used in Herr Adam's offices. Moreover, on ESP tests she did not score much higher than chance would permit.

The range of PK and poltergeist activity that occurred in Rosenheim was astonishingly wide, and the case remains one of the most thoroughly documented in modern times. Permanent records still are preserved of the TV films, photographs, and videotapes taken by the networks and Dr. Bender's team of investigators, as are the tabulated records of the voltage and telephone apparatus. Although the causes of the PK activity are only partly comprehended, the Rosenheim case stands as one of the very few in which poltergeist phenomena activated a system of telephones.

INDIA

THE POLTERGEIST
OF BOMBAY PROVINCE

MANY PSYCHIC INVESTIGATORS HAVE BEEN INTERESTED IN
the poltergeist that manifested itself in a small city just south
of Bombay in India. Among them were the Englishman
Harry Price and Father Herbert Thurston, a Jesuit priest
who spent much of his life probing poltergeist phenomena.
The full details of the disturbances, which lasted for several
years, were officially published in the *British Journal for Psychical Research*.

While most poltergeist cases seem associated with restless
or upset teenagers, these events centered around an eight-
year-old boy named Damodar Bapat, an orphan. The boy's
mother, who had been bothered by odd visions, had taken

her own life. Damodar's father, a high-caste Brahmin, had died shortly after the boy's birth in 1920.

Dr. S. V. Ketkar, another Brahmin gentleman, and his German wife adopted Damodar shortly after his father's death. The Ketkars were highly respected citizens and intellectuals. When the disturbances began in their home during the mid-1920s, a physician friend, Dr. J. D. Jenkins, reported that the couple started to "suffer terribly . . . both in name, in estate, and in all their affairs." Because of the upsetting poltergeist disturbances, the Ketkars' health began to fail, and they found that servants would seldom remain long in the troubled house.

At length Dr. Jenkins, at the urging of the Ketkars, agreed to come into their home to give his professional opinion of the queer happenings, which included objects being flung about, things appearing out of nowhere, and personal property suddenly being smashed as if by an unseen and malevolent hand. After moving into the house, Dr. Jenkins interviewed various eyewitnesses who had been present when the annoyances occurred. It did not take the doctor long to find out that they nearly always happened when young Damodar was about.

In order to observe and study the boy for awhile, Jenkins isolated Damodar in one of the rooms of the Ketkars' residence. The physician put the youth—completely naked—on a small bed, took his pulse, and instructed him to just lie there quietly. Jenkins then closed the door and the windows, draped a sheet over Damodar, and sat down in a far corner of the room to see if anything unnatural would happen. The doctor did not have long to wait. After a few minutes, the doctor was amazed to witness the sheet jerked off the lad and the bed move into the center of the room—all by itself. At this point, Damodar was elevated off the bed and deposited gently on the floor. Later the boy told the doctor that he could actually feel the arms of some invisible being lifting him.

Next, the perplexed Jenkins observed a bottle of ink on a nearby desk leave its resting place and come sailing through the air directly at him. Luckily, it narrowly missed his head. This was followed by a barrage of Damodar's toys being thrown about the room. The doctor told the parents about these odd events; it was his opinion that they could not be attributed to pranks by the boy or any other physical causes.

The next day Dr. Jenkins came to the Ketkars' house with some skeptical friends. One was a policeman and another was, in Jenkins' own words, "an irascible old major, who had settled the whole problem by the simple process of calling me a liar when I related to him the happenings of the day before." That afternoon the doctor saw some more of the unaccountable phenomena. Once, as everyone was chatting on the veranda, a small table, untouched by anyone, came "hobbling" across the floor. It headed directly for the major, imprisoning him temporarily in his armchair.

At dinner that same evening, other strange things started to occur. A salt cellar began to dance crazily about the table. The major's glass fell over all by itself. Next, the whole table was cleared by unseen hands. This was too much for the major. He muttered "Good night" and left the table. Dr. Jenkins recorded these and dozens of other odd events in a diary that he kept during his investigation for the Ketkars. Most of these events were later published.

During the early months of 1928, Dr. Ketkar's sister-in-law Miss H. Kohn was living with the family, and she too recorded some of the odd disturbances. This young woman was a teacher of European languages at Bombay University, and her notes, which she sent to Father Thurston in Eng-

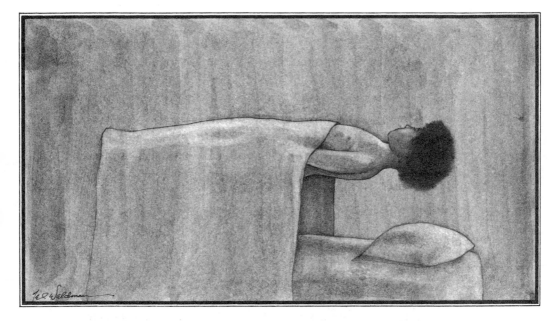

land, covered a period of eleven months. "I took especial care," she wrote to Thurston, "to avoid the slightest exaggeration or inaccuracy, and the events were always recorded immediately after their occurrence." Miss Kohn also said that many people suspected Damodar of producing the disturbances. But the more she observed the events, the more she became convinced that the boy was quite innocent of participating in them in any way.

One Sunday in July 1928, Miss Kohn was standing in her bedroom talking with Damodar when a small glass jar of vegetable extract was hurled into the room. The jar had been standing in the dining room with some others in a closed cupboard. In order for the jar to have reached the bedroom— where it forthwith smashed to pieces—it had had to turn a corner! The boy could not possibly have hurled it himself.

Curiously, this poltergeist seemed to have a deep aversion to ink. Nearly every ink container in the Ketkar household was either smashed or spilled. Once Miss Kohn was having dinner with the Ketkars in their dining room; Damodar was also present, but he happened to step into one of the bedrooms for a few seconds. At that moment, a screw-top jar of ink that Dr. Ketkar had managed to keep safely until then came sailing through the dining room and into the bedroom where the boy was standing. There it broke, spilling the ink onto the floor. Incredibly, this missile had been transported all the way from Dr. Ketkar's study in the extreme front of the house!

Another time a visitor had called to see Dr. Ketkar. As Miss Kohn was fetching a pad and pencil that he had asked for, an aspirin bottle from a shelf in the dining room was suddenly hurled in her direction by, as she later wrote, "an invisible hand." The bottle flew at her with such excellent aim that she screamed with terror. Yet when it reached her, it merely fell at her feet without breaking. All the while, Damodar was standing quietly near her.

As time went by, Dr. Ketkar and his family grew more depressed about the weird happenings in their house. They were careful not to publicize them, for they felt this would only bring more trouble from suspicious and alarmed neighbors. Their greatest hope was to find some way to bring the violent events to an end. So damaging had their unseen intruder grown that sometimes the family could not be sure they had enough food on hand for the next meal. The poltergeist evidently disliked eggs as well as ink. Once Mrs. Ketkar brought home four dozen eggs and put them away in a large basket in the dining room cupboard. No sooner had she done so than an egg from the direction of the *closed* cupboard flew toward the two women and smashed on the floor. They took the basket out of the cupboard and counted the eggs. One was missing. Miss Kohn cleaned up the mess, but immediately another egg shot toward them from the opposite direction—that is, *not* from the direction of the cupboard. Again the eggs were counted and a second egg was now missing. Both women had been watching Damodar during this event, but not once had the boy come near the cupboard.

On another occasion Mrs. Ketkar noticed that a heavy lock on a cupboard in her room was hanging open; only minutes before she had locked it herself. She had chosen to inspect this lock for a very good reason. As she had crossed the dining room only a minute or two before, a large empty basket was flung at her head from above. This basket was the same one that she had locked away in the cupboard in her room.

Sometimes the poltergeist could be as humorous as it was annoying. One morning Miss Kohn was planning to go out, but first decided that her shoes needed polishing. However, she was unable to locate the shoe polish which was missing from its usual place on a shelf. Irritated, she questioned every member of the household, but everyone denied having seen it. Deciding to go without polishing her shoes, she was in the act of putting on her hat when she was startled by a sudden thud. It was the missing can of polish, which apparently had come from some point in midair and landed right at her feet. Again, the boy was present in the room, but from where he was sitting he could have had nothing to do with the event. The next morning exactly the same thing happened. The shoe polish was missing. This time Miss Kohn simply called out, "Shoe polish, please!" The can came to her in the same gentle manner as before.

The poltergeist also appeared to enjoy making off with money. Bills were even taken from locked receptacles. Sometimes the money was never recovered. At other times, the exact amount would be returned—but in small change! "On several occasions in broad daylight," wrote Miss Kohn, "we saw coins fall among us from above. This was always while the boy was in the house. . . . At first we could not always see the coins in midair, but merely saw them fall. . . . Soon, however, we actually saw the money appear in the air. . . . In some cases these seemed to be coins which were missing from our purses; in other cases we could not account for the coins. In every instance, it was most obvious that the boy himself was not doing the mischief."

One day Miss Kohn left her handbag containing a change purse in the dining room. In the purse were two rupees. Returning for it later, she located the bag, but the purse was missing from it. Again the resourceful Miss Kohn demanded her property: "Purse, please!" Whereupon the purse fell gently at her feet. The two rupees, however, were not in it, nor were they ever returned.

This Indian poltergeist evidently objected as strongly as its brother ghosts to the rite of exorcism. Once a priest came to say a mantra, and immediately a large china cup was smashed to pieces in the dining room. But finally—and mercifully—the intruder tired of causing havoc in the household and seemed to lose its psychic force. In the later months of 1930, the disturbances subsided and peace returned once more to the Ketkar family.

THE STONE-THROWING GHOST OF SUMATRA

WHILE INSTANCES OF STONE-THROWING POLTERGEISTS have been reported just about everywhere in the world, they appear to be more prevalent in certain global areas. One of these regions is the Andes chain in Peru, where families and sometimes entire villages have been disturbed by falling chunks of adobe, cobblestones, pieces of tile, lumps of mud, and other objects. Another stone-throwing location is Sumatra, in the former Dutch East Indies, today known as Indonesia. Inhabitants of the large island are accustomed to these disturbances, and they are often reported in their newspapers. The late naturalist and psychic researcher Ivan Sanderson once actually played "catch" with some airborne stones on Sumatra.

One of the most remarkable cases of a stone-throwing poltergeist anywhere was recounted by a Dutch engineer in 1903 in the steaming jungles of Sumatra. One respected

English psychic researcher called it "one of the best observed and most striking cases in history." Another investigator has said that "it qualifies as one of the leading poltergeist cases of the early twentieth century." It is considered all the more authentic because the engineer, W. D. Grottendieck of Dordrecht, Holland, was much interested in science and inclined to be a skeptic in occult matters. His personal account of the occurrences was later published in the British *Journal of the Society for Psychical Research* in 1906.

One day in September 1903, the Dutchman returned to his camp after a long trek through the jungles with some fifty Sumatran coolies. Grottendieck worked for a Dutch oil company, and this had been one of the exploratory trips he made from time to time. When he got back to camp, the engineer discovered that his regular quarters had been temporarily taken by another member of the company. He had to put up his bed in a new house that had just been erected on bamboo poles.

The roof of what was to become that night a "haunted hut" was of typical Sumatran jungle construction. It was thatched by large dried leaves, known in Sumatrese as *kadjang*, which overlapped each other, shingle fashion. These leaves, measuring about two by three feet, are very hard and have tough fibers. Grottendieck, worn out from his long march, hastily laid out his sleeping bag and mosquito netting directly on the hut's wooden floor and dropped off to sleep immediately.

Later, about one o'clock in the morning, he half awoke, after hearing something fall near his head outside the netting. Two or three minutes later, he became fully awake and tried to see what it could be that was falling on the floor beside him. Soon he realized that they were small black stones, all less than an inch in size. The engineer then arose and turned up his kerosene lamp. In the illumination, he was astonished to see that the little black stones seemed to be falling right through the tough kadjang roofing down onto the floor next to his pillow. Wondering what in the world could be the cause of this mystifying bombardment, the Dutchman went into the next room and woke up his Malay servant boy.

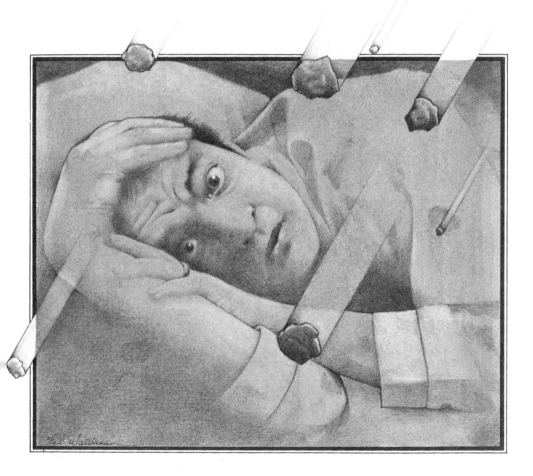

Grottendieck instructed him to go outside the hut and find
out whether somebody was playing a prank on him. While
the boy was making his search, the engineer held a small
flashlight for him; he noted that the tiny stones did not stop
falling inside the hut—they seemed to go straight through
the roofing. When the boy returned without having found
anything amiss, he was told to search the kitchen.

The Dutchman then went back inside the sleeping room
to watch the odd falling stones again. He knelt down near his
pillow and tried to catch a few of them as they floated
through the air toward him. Curiously, he found himself
unable to catch a single one! No sooner did he think he had
grasped one than it changed direction in midair and veered
away. Although they eluded his hands, they still continued
to strike the floor beside him.

At this juncture the mystified Grottendieck decided to
clamber up the partition between his room and the boy's in
order to examine the roof just above—the place from which
the tiny stones seemed to be emanating. While he could
clearly see the stones coming right through the sturdy kadjang leaves, he could spot no holes in them. Moreover, when
he attempted to catch the stones at the point where they
emerged from the leaves, he could not do so. After he had
climbed down again, his servant boy returned to announce
that there was no one in the kitchen. Still believing that a
friend was playing some sort of practical joke on him, the
Dutchman grabbed his Mauser rifle and, from the boy's
room, fired five rounds into the air above the jungle. In this
way he hoped to startle the trickster into revealing himself.
But the stones, which were still falling intermittently, failed
to stop.

After Grottendieck fired the shots, the Malay boy looked
into the room where his master had been sleeping, and for
the first time he too observed the falling stones. Thoroughly

frightened, he told the engineer that Satan was the cause of it, and then fled into the darkness of the jungle. Grottendieck never saw him again. Furthermore, after the lad's departure, the stones ceased to fall—a fact that suggests the boy himself was probably the energy focus for the disturbances. When the Dutchman knelt to examine the stones, he felt that they were warm to the touch. Still baffled, he went back to his sleeping bag and dropped off again.

The next morning, Grottendieck discovered everything as he had left it the night before. On the floor near the boy's window lay the five expended cartridge shells. Strangely, however, he could locate only about two dozen of the little black stones. Again he examined the roof, but could see no hole or even a crack in the tough leaves. It crossed the Dutchman's mind that the stones, being warm the night before, might have been small meteorites; however, he did not see how this could be possible since they almost certainly would have torn holes in the roof.

After the engineer had reported the odd affair to the Society for Psychical Research, some officers of that body who had become highly interested in the case wrote back to him posing a number of questions. Point by point, the Dutchman answered them. Here are his answers in his own words:

1. All around the house was *jungle*, in front, behind, to the left and to the right.

2. There was no other soul in the house and kitchen than myself and the boy.

3. The boy certainly did *not* do it, because at the same time I bent over him, while he was sleeping on the floor, to awaken him, there fell a couple of stones. I not only *saw* them fall on the floor in the room but I also *heard* them fall, the door being at the moment half open.

4. While the boy was standing *in front of me* and I shot my

cartridges, at the same moment, I heard the stones fall behind me.

5. I climbed up the poles of the roof and I saw quite distinctly that the stones came right through the kadjang.

6. The stones (though not all of them) were hotter than could be explained by their having been kept in the hand or pocket for some time.

7. All the stones without exception fell down within a certain radius of not more than 3 feet; they all came through the same kadjang leaf (that is, all the ones I saw) and they all fell down within the same radius on the floor.

8. They fell rather slowly. Now, supposing that somebody might by trickery have forced them through the roof, or supposing they had not come through at all—even then there would remain something mysterious about it, because it seemed to me that they were *hovering* through the air; they described a parabolic line that then came down with a bang on the floor.

9. The sound they made in falling down on the floor was also abnormal, because considering their slow motion the bang was much too loud.

At many of the Society's subsequent meetings, the strange case was discussed and rediscussed. More letters were written to the engineer requesting clarification of certain points. Dutifully the Dutchman wrote back, repeating his reasons for believing the boy could not possibly have thrown the stones without being detected. Like so many other poltergeist cases, it has remained unsolved. Grottendieck himself wrote the final chapter to the affair in a letter to the Society: "I am afraid that the whole thing will ever remain a puzzle to me."

IRELAND

THE COFFIN CARRIER
OF TULLAMORE

LORD DUFFERIN'S STRANGE AND FASCINATING STORY FIRST began at a country estate called Tullamore, not far from the Irish seaport of Wexford. Lord Dufferin, a distinguished British diplomat, was not an especially imaginative man. What reason would he have had to invent such a tale? At any rate, the apparition—if such it was—that he saw one night at Tullamore doubtless saved his life.

Lord Dufferin had had almost a storybook career. At the age of fifteen he had succeeded to the title of Baron Dufferin and Clandeboye in the Irish peerage. His first important diplomatic success was as British representative in negotiations at Constantinople over the massacre of the Christians in Syria. Created an earl in 1871, he became governor-general of Canada the following year. After serving as ambassador to Russia and Turkey, he was viceroy of India from 1884 to 1888. In the latter year, he was created marquess of Dufferin and Ava, and in 1889 he was named ambassador to Italy. Now back in Ireland for a rest, he was relaxing as a house guest of an old friend, the owner of Tullamore. The year was 1890.

On this night that he would never forget, Lord Dufferin said good night to his host and climbed the great staircase to his bedchamber. As he entered the room, he was in a mellow mood from enjoying good food, good drink, and good friends. A cheery log fire in the spacious fireplace further enhanced his feeling of ease and tranquility. He prepared for bed, and then decided to read for a while.

After about twenty minutes, he closed the book and put it aside. Extinguishing the gaslight near his bed, he catnapped for a bit, but found himself oddly restless and unable to sleep. This was rare, for he usually fell directly asleep and slumbered soundly until morning. After twisting and turning, he felt so uneasy and disturbed that he got out of bed. Going to the window, he gazed out over the rolling moonlit lawns of Tullamore. There were no clouds and the light of the moon drenched the neat paths, cropped shrubbery, and sumptuous gardens below his casement window. All seemed perfectly motionless and the nobleman just stood there for several minutes taking in the loveliness of the nocturnal scene.

Then abruptly Lord Dufferin saw a movement that broke the stillness. Watching fascinated, he saw the figure of a man step out of a long shadow into the moonlight. Quietly and deliberately, the figure strode directly across the rolling lawn. The nobleman could see that the mysterious man was nearly bent double under the weight of a long and ponderous box on his back. When the bearer of this burden reached the center of the lawn, bringing him into clear view of the watching Lord Dufferin, he paused, lifted his head, and stared straight at the noted diplomat.

The moonlight now revealed the full features of the man as his eyes met Lord Dufferin's. So terrible was the face to look at that the nobleman shuddered and recoiled a step or two backward. Dufferin was later to describe the face as "full of horror and malevolence." Turning away, the bearer of the burden continued his way across the lawn until he was lost to view in clumps of shrubbery. Only then did it dawn on Lord Dufferin that the man's heavy burden was a coffin.

After a few seconds, Lord Dufferin turned away from the window and looked at his watch. It was well past one o'clock and everyone else in the house appeared to be asleep. Everything was as still and quiet as death. Once again he returned to the window; all was as motionless as it had been before the appearance of the coffin carrier. Not a breath of wind stirred the silent scene. There was little doubt in Dufferin's mind that he had seen an actual person trek across the lawn. He had even cast a shadow, the nobleman had noticed. Even so, there had been an eerie specterlike quality about the figure. Then suddenly Dufferin realized he was cold and shivering. Baffled by what he had seen, he returned to bed and slept well for the remainder of the night.

The following morning at breakfast, Lord Dufferin related his weird experience of the early morning hours to his host and other guests. But nobody seemed to take seriously his account of the hideously ugly figure bearing a coffin across the lawn.

In 1891 Lord Dufferin became the ambassador to France, a post that he filled for the next few years. One morning he was scheduled to give a talk to an influential group of diplo-

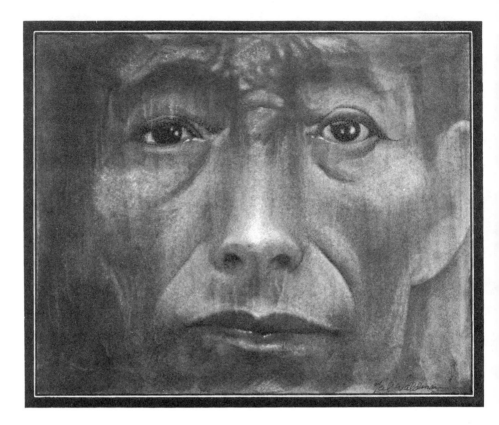

mats on the fifth floor of a Paris hotel. When he arrived, he and his secretary were ushered by the hotel manager to the elevator.

Finally the elevator shuddered to a stop in the main lobby and the doors opened. Dufferin was talking to his secretary and scarcely paid attention to the fact that a number of people boarded the elevator ahead of him. Then the secretary, seeing the elevator was about to close without them, motioned to his superior to step inside.

Lord Dufferin stepped forward, and saw the uniformed elevator operator for the first time. The man was facing him and staring straight at him. Dumbfounded and shocked, Dufferin recoiled as he had done at Tullamore, automatically stepping back out of the elevator. The face of the operator was the same tortured face he had seen that night in Ireland carrying the coffin across the lawn.

Once again Dufferin felt the clammy fear he had known on that night. Shaken with disbelief, he waved the elevator away, much to the astonishment of the hotel manager. As he uncertainly waited for it to come down again, he heard a sudden loud clang, then a series of thundering banging sounds. These were punctuated with a horrible screech and finally by a terrible bone-crunching thud that reverberated through the entire hotel.

Later Dufferin learned what had occurred. The elevator had just reached the fifth floor—his own destination—but its doors never opened there. The faulty suspension cable had snapped, and the loaded elevator had plunged sickeningly downward and crashed at the bottom of the shaft. Five passengers died in the accident, among them the operator whose hideous face had prevented Lord Dufferin from stepping aboard the ill-fated elevator. When Dufferin made inquiries about the operator, he learned that the man had been hired for that day only, replacing the regular operator. No one knew his name nor where he had come from.

Lord Dufferin died in Ireland at Clandeboye in the year 1902. His grandson, a subsequent Marquess of Dufferin and Ava, once remarked about the strange matter: "The story is perfectly true, but my grandfather could never explain it. We have always believed the tale and were puzzled about it, since grandfather did not believe in ghosts."

THE WHISPERING
GHOST OF VERCELLI

TITO SCHIPA—THE FAMOUS OPERA SINGER BORN IN LECCE,
Italy, in 1890—was known for the sweetness and lyricism of
his voice. Trained for five years by the renowned Maestro
Gerunda, Tito made his operatic debut in *La Traviata* and
became a success overnight. In 1919 after singing in numerous Spanish and South American cities, he went to America
to become the leading tenor for the Chicago Opera Company. Thousands flocked to see and hear him in such works
as *Barber of Seville, Lakmé, Lucia,* and *Tosca*. But only a few of
Tito's intimates ever knew that he had had several psychic
experiences.

One of these occurred when he was a young boy. Lying in
bed one night, unable to sleep, Tito was amazed to see at the
foot of his bed an apparition of a beautiful woman. She was

wearing a Spanish veil and carried a fan. Tito saw her lips move as if she wished to say something to him, but he could hear no words. Then, very slowly, the apparition simply faded away before his eyes. Tito thought this a very strange occurrence, and he told his mother about it. But his mother pooh-poohed the boy's story and told him he had merely been dreaming.

A few months later, Tito paid a visit to his uncle in Parma, where he had never been before. One day Tito happened to be glancing through his uncle's family album of photographs with his mother, who had come with him to Parma. Presently the boy came to a picture of his uncle's recently deceased wife; it had been taken in Spain at the time of their marriage.

"Mama!" he exclaimed. "Look! This lady—she is the one I saw that night!"

Tito had never seen his uncle's wife, nor had he ever seen a picture of her. His uncle and mother questioned the boy closely about what he had seen. Soon it was ascertained that Tito had seen the lady's ghost on the same night as her death.

Even more interesting was another incident that happened in Tito's early days of opera singing. It occurred in the town of Vercelli, where he had first made his debut in La Traviata. Tito was staying at an inn—a very old one—and he noticed that a strange atmosphere of gloom hung over the place. This somberness seemed to affect the entire personnel of the tavern—from the manager down to the stable boys.

In time Tito learned the reason. Everyone, including the manager, was afraid that the inn might have to be sold, and they would all lose their positions. For generations, the ancient tavern had always been inherited by the owner's eldest son, whose early life was spent in learning how to operate and manage the establishment. However, the father of the present manager and eldest son had died and left no will. Because there was no will, according to Italian law the inn would have to be sold and the proceeds divided equally among the dead man's heirs.

At one point the inn became very crowded and the manager asked Tito if he would mind giving up his large room to a married couple and take a smaller one. Tito liked the young man and said that he would not mind at all. The manager then told him that the only room he had left was the small one in which his father had died. Would that bother Tito at all? Tito replied that he had no foolish fears on that score and he moved into it. On his first night in the room, he slept soundly until the morning.

On the second night he was not so lucky. Tossing fitfully for hours, Tito at last managed to drop off to sleep. Suddenly he was awakened by a whirring noise that sounded like a big bird circling just above his head. Believing that a bat had flown in through the open window, Tito got up, lit a candle, and searched about the room. He could find no bird or bat at all.

Returning to bed, Tito again fell asleep. But in the half-dawn he was once more aroused by a repetition of the eerie whirring noise just above his head. Only partially conscious, Tito came fully awake when he clearly heard some spoken words. The voice, sounding husky and uttering the words singly, said, "Look-on-left-wall." The last word was almost inaudible. Whether Tito had dreamed this or really heard it he did not know for certain. At any rate, he arose and looked around in the dim light. The left wall of the room appeared to him no different from any of the other walls. It was wainscotted from floor to ceiling with oak paneling, and upon it hung an old oil painting.

Tito smiled to himself at what seemed like a figment of his imagination and crawled back into bed. No sooner had he done so than he heard three sharp knocks against the wooden wainscotting of the left wall. Deciding that the disturbance must be due to a bat that was blindly seeking its freedom, Tito got up once again. This time he began to search more thoroughly, for he was annoyed at having his rest interrupted.

Tito's next thought was that the bat or bird or whatever it was had gotten itself trapped behind the old painting. Dragging a table across the room, he climbed up on it and took down the picture. He saw that it was a rendition of the martyrdom of St. Sebastian—a cruel and somber one showing the bleeding wounds and arrows piercing the saint's body. Tito then turned the picture around and leaned the face of it against the wainscotting. There was no bat or bird or any other creature to be seen on the back of it at all.

Before Tito climbed back up on the table to rehang the picture, something caught his eye. The daylight was getting stronger and he saw the gleam of a piece of white paper. It was neatly folded and stuck in the back of the oil painting between the wooden stretcher and the canvas. Pulling the paper out, Tito took it to a window to investigate. It proved to be the lost will, leaving the inn to the eldest son!

At that moment Tito felt himself break out in a cold sweat. The will dropped from his hands. His first thought was that the voice speaking to him must have been that of the dead father. Then Tito's reason began to refute this idea. Possibly, his mind preoccupied with the story of the will, he had merely dreamed those words, or, half awake, had simply imagined them. As for the whirring, knocking sounds, they might have been made by a bat or bird that had since flown away.

But Tito was also a singer, and he was keenly sensitive in his response to surrounding influences. Often he found he was able to read the thoughts of those around him, much as an antenna of a radio receives sounds. He was also, he knew, possessed of psychic abilities. Might not that same sensitive response to the hidden paper have inspired him, driven on by the half-dream, to the finding of the will? Whatever the explanation, there was the will, and his friend the manager was a happy man when Tito turned it over to him.

THE WHITE LADY
OF YOKOSUKA

Multiple-witness cases involving apparitions are comparatively rare in psychical research. Their value lies in the fact that more than one observer has seen a ghostly form, thus confirming that what one person saw others saw as well. One such case occurred shortly after World War II, when crewmen aboard a United States destroyer witnessed the same phantom while tied up at the United States Naval Base at Yokosuka in outer Tokyo Bay.

In the summer of 1947 the destroyer lay alongside one of the many piers that accommodated American naval vessels at the Yokosuka base in Occupied Japan. The dock was a high one, actually built to berth larger ships, so that when the men went ashore from the ship, they walked up the gangway instead of down. From the deck of the low-lying destroyer it was possible to see people on the long pier above only if they were standing or walking fairly near the planking at the pier's edge. It was here that the apparition was seen by most of the crew. The destroyer had just finished a tour of picket duty with a small aircraft carrier; now she was in port for a three weeks' refitting, and the men were given plenty of liberty ashore. Although the destroyer returned afterwards to the same pier, the apparition was never seen again.

It was on the third night in port that the phantom was first observed. During the mid-watch from midnight to 0400 hours, a wild-eyed young torpedoman burst into the quarterdeck area and began babbling to the Officer of the Deck that he had seen a ghost "sort of floating along," as he put it, on the pier above as he was standing his watch.

The officer told the young sailor to calm down and tell him exactly what he had seen. Was it still there? No, the young man said, it had just glided down the long pier, past the ship, and then "just kind of melted away." What had it looked like? the Officer of the Deck wanted to know.

The sailor, calmer now, explained that it was clearly the figure of a woman—by the look of her hairdo and dress, a Japanese woman. He said that he had first caught sight of her as she came abreast of the ship, and that her form was transparent; he was able to see right through her as she glided on by. The officer then asked if there was anything else he had noticed about the figure. Yes, the sailor replied, she was dressed in what seemed to be some kind of white ceremonial kimono with a wide obi sash around her waist. Anything else? the officer asked. Yes, sir, answered the young man. She was carrying something in her hands: a perfectly square box, perhaps a foot square in all dimensions, and it too was white and tied with a dark ribbon.

The officer took the boy back out on deck and told him to show him where he'd been standing when he saw the ghost. The sailor indicated a spot nearly opposite the turret of the 4-inch forward gun. He pointed up to the pier where he had first seen the apparition, then arced his finger along to the place where the phantom had melted away. No one was on the pier now—neither human nor ghost—and all that could be seen above the piling was the blue-black Japanese night sky. The officer shrugged and told the sailor to continue standing his watch. If he saw the figure again or anything else suspicious, he said, he was to report it immediately. But nothing further was seen that night.

Two nights later, a chief bosun's mate—an older man— was having a smoke on the foredeck before turning in. It was after midnight and he couldn't seem to get to sleep. He had not been ashore that night and was perfectly sober. Just as he flicked his cigarette over the side, he happened to look up toward the looming pier. He later told the duty officer that he was astonished to see a Japanese lady dressed in white gliding along the edge of the pier. He swore he could see right through her. She had, the chief said, carried some kind of square box in her hands with a ribbon around it. "So help me, sir," he said, "it was a real ghost!" Then, he continued, he had watched the white figure glide along the pier and slowly fade from view. The chief had seen essentially the same figure as the torpedoman two nights before.

Three nights after this, a young gunner's mate came off liberty, checked in with the officer at the quarterdeck, and he too strolled forward for a last cigarette before hitting the sack. He had had a couple of beers at a local tavern in Yokosuka but no more than that. Walking out the long pier to the ship, he had seen no one and he had come aboard alone. No sooner had he lit his cigarette than he happened to glance up at the old pilings and froze at what he saw. Like the other two men, he distinctly saw the phantom lady glide past the ship atop the pier carrying her square box. He watched the white figure simply melt away and then dutifully reported what he had seen to the Officer of the Deck.

It was not long before the "scuttlebutt" about the mysterious White Lady, as she came to be called by the sailors, spread throughout the ship. The three witnesses got together and checked their stories with each other. Each had seen the specter gliding along the pier; each had seen her carrying the box; and each had seen the figure slowly fade away. Eventually word of the White Lady reached the ears of the captain, who thought it might be worthwhile to convene an informal board of officers to listen to the men's stories one by one. This was done, and so earnestly did each man relate his story that the board saw no reason to doubt their word.

By this time just about everybody aboard was eager to get a glimpse of the ghostly White Lady. Knots of curious men—officers included—gathered along the rails after midnight; all eyes peered upward along the length of the pier searching diligently for any movement. Not a thing was seen for the next five nights, and soon many of the men lost interest. But a dozen or so were still watching on the sixth night when the White Lady put in her next appearance. Some sailors made low whistles and whispered to each other as they witnessed the apparition above them glide majestically along the pier, clutching her square box, and then fade into nothingness. All agreed that the whole performance had taken less than a minute. Some commented that the phantom seemed to have a "sorrowful look" on her gauzy, transparent face.

At any rate, this multiple-witness occurrence rekindled everybody's interest in the ghost. Every man who was off duty after midnight crowded the starboard side of the destroyer's deck, their accumulated weight putting a slight list on the ship. On-duty cooks, engineroom men, and other belowdecks personnel traded off portions of their work shifts to get a few minutes on deck to watch for the ghost. The ship's PA system was used minimally during these hours so as not to "scare off" the phantom lady. Nothing happened for the next four nights. In fact, though no one of course knew it at the time, the specter would show up only once more to the destroyer's crew. When she did, it was with a new variation.

Three more nights passed and nothing was seen. On the fourth night all hands who were not on duty grew tense as the ship's bell sounded midnight. Men crowded the starboard rails and some perched themselves a few feet up the gangway—but not too far lest their presence "jinx" the ghost and scare it away. Aloft on the pier there was no one. Many sailors had a gut feeling that this would be the night and had put money on it. Since the phantom's last appearance, no fewer than three "White Lady pools" had been formed, and their pots had grown considerably. Forty-five minutes went by and the men smoked nervously and talked in hushed whispers. Soon the ship's bell chimed 0100 hours.

Precisely seven minutes later, somebody whispered loudly, "There she comes!" And indeed, the now familiar figure of the White Lady was visible on the pier approaching the ship's fan-tail. The men watched her glide quickly along, holding her box gingerly as before. Soon the phantom was directly amidships. The fascinated sailors gaped in silence at the gauzy apparition and held their breaths.

Suddenly one crewman whispered loudly, "Look, there's *another* ghost!"

All eyes swung to a position several feet beyond the destroyer's bow. There on the pier's edge stood what appeared to be the filmy outline of a Japanese soldier. He was holding out his arms to the approaching White Lady in a gesture of humble entreaty—or so it looked to the watching sailors. But the White Lady just glided on, oblivious, and seemed to the men to pass through the form of the ghostly soldier. The latter was then observed to turn slightly, still supplicating the White Lady with his outstretched arms. In a few seconds both figures faded slowly from view, never to be seen again by the destroyer's crew.

During the last few days in port, the ship buzzed with talk about the strange event. The men traded stories to see whether any of them had seen something different from the others. But everyone had seen the identical pageant of events. A hopeful vigil was still kept after midnight by many men, but in vain. With new picket duty orders, the ship was soon back out to sea. The cruise lasted for eight weeks, and when word was passed that their ship would again tie up at the same pier in Yokosuka, the men speculated on the chance of getting another glimpse of the White Lady. But no one aboard ever saw her again.

Back in port one evening, just two days before his ship was slated for sea duty again, the captain was having a drink with a fellow officer at the Officers' Club. The captain had been telling him about the odd appearances of the ghostly lady. The fellow officer thought awhile and then suggested the captain might have a talk with the old harbormaster at Yokosuka, who might possibly know something about the strange affair.

Out of curiosity the captain did so. The old harbormaster nodded understandingly as the American officer related what he and his men had seen. Yes, he himself had once seen the same spectral figure from his patrol boat after midnight.

"Harbormaster-*san*," said the captain, using the Japanese respectful form of address, "do you know what it means?"

The old Japanese man nodded. During the war, he said, this same pier had several times been used to unload dead

Japanese servicemen, many of whom had been cremated. A mass ceremony for the dead had usually been held on the pier, and mothers, wives, and other relatives had afterward come to claim their men's bodies or carry away the boxes of their ashes. Possibly, speculated the harbormaster, the White Lady had been one of these women. Perhaps, he continued, she herself was now dead and haunted the pier in a reenactment of the grief she had felt on that day. Of the phantom soldier, who knew? Perhaps he had been her dead son or husband, whose spirit had been present when she had claimed the box containing his ashes.

Later the puzzled captain debated with himself whether he should share this macabre information with his officers and crew. Finally he decided against it. Why get them all stirred up again? Besides, he wanted their minds clear for their next tour of sea duty.

NORWAY

THE VARDØGER GHOST OF OSLO

PSYCHIC INVESTIGATORS HAVE ALWAYS BEEN BAFFLED BY so-called "arrival" cases. In such cases, a person (or persons) is seen by others to "arrive" at a place before he or she actually gets there in the flesh. In Norway, for some reason, arrival phenomena are fairly common occurrences. They are called *Vardøger*, or "forerunners." For instance, a man is heard or seen by his family to arrive home; he may hang up his hat, light his pipe, even say hello—then he disappears. A few minutes later, he really does arrive, this time in the flesh. The family thinks nothing of the preliminary occurrence, knowing it simply means that Dad is due to arrive home soon and it's all right for Mom to start the dinner.

While a number of theories have been advanced to explain the ghostly *Vardøger* arrivals, none have really done so satisfactorily. Of them, two are more plausible than the rest. The first concerns the theory of *astral projection*, also known as *exteriorization* or *out-of-body experience*. According to this theory, there is a temporary separation of the astral or second or spirit body from the physical body. In *Vardøger* cases, the person in question is thinking intensely of the place to which he is going—usually a pleasant place, such as home, where comforts and loved ones await him. He strongly anticipates his arrival and what he will do when he gets there. In so doing, he unconsciously wills his second or spirit body to separate from his physical one and project to his destination. His physical self may, for instance, be trapped on a long, boring train ride or faced with another half hour's walking time before his arrival. But his second body, momentarily willed free and unencumbered by either physical matter or time, arrives instantly at the longed-for destination. There, in some way, it briefly takes on the materialized quality of an apparition, then vanishes again.

The second theory suggests that somehow the element of time is out of joint. In other words, the *Vardøger* occurrence is a duplication of an event in time. The coming event takes place twice—once in a preliminary time, then again at its own time. But the *Vardøger* ghost of the man involved in this case involved a new variation on the arrival case; namely, a larger gap in time between events.

During the summer of 1955, Erkson Gorique, a successful American importer, decided to go to Norway to investigate the purchase of some china and glassware in that country. A widely traveled businessman, Gorique had never been to Norway, though for several years he had declared his intention of visiting the land of the fjords. But something else had always come up, and he had kept on postponing the trip until 1955.

Arriving at Oslo in July, he asked where he might find the best hotel in the city. Then he took a taxi directly there. Gorique, it must be emphasized, knew no one in Oslo or, in fact, in the whole of Norway.

As Gorique signed the register at the hotel's desk, the room clerk smiled pleasantly at him and remarked, "I'm so glad to see you again, Mr. Gorique. It's very good to have you back."

Astonished, the importer replied, "I'm sorry, but you must be mistaking me for someone else. I've never been here before."

The clerk, however, insisted that he had been in the hotel a few months previously and had made his July reservation at that time. It was, the clerk told Gorique, his rather unusual name and American appearance that had stuck in his mind.

"But it just can't be so," Gorique protested. "I've never even been in Norway before."

"Then, sir," the clerk said, catching a glimpse of the hotel manager looking his way, "I must be mistaken. I do hope you'll forgive me."

Matters grew more puzzling for Erkson Gorique when he visited the wholesale dealer whom he had planned to see about the glassware and china. Mr. Olsen, a friendly white-haired man, rose from behind his desk and offered the American a hearty handclasp.

Before Gorique could speak, Mr. Olsen exclaimed, "How wonderful that you did get back, Mr. Gorique. You were in such a hurry last time that we weren't able to conclude the final details of our business."

Completely stunned, Gorique slumped back into a chair in Mr. Olsen's office. Surely, he thought, the man must be

taking him for someone else, just as the room clerk had.

"Tell me," queried the American, "when was I here last?"

"Why," Olsen answered, looking perplexed, "it was just a few months back."

With a sigh of resignation, Erkson Gorique appealed to the Norwegian glass dealer. He explained that he had never been to Norway in his entire life before—and that he could prove it. Yet, he added, everywhere he went, hotel clerks, waiters, and now he, Mr. Olsen, recognized him and spoke of former visits.

Mr. Olsen listened carefully to Erkson Gorique's story without interruption. When he had finished, he began to explain to him about the Norwegian *Vardøger*. To the American, it all sounded like a fantastic fairy tale.

"I can offer you no concrete explanation for our *Vardøger*," Mr. Olsen concluded, "but it is not such a rare thing as psychic phenomena go, at least not here in Norway. You really shouldn't let the experience upset you too much."

POLTERGEIST
OF THE ANDES

DURING THE 1930S, A YOUNG AMERICAN MINING ENGINEER named Jack Baragwanath spent a number of years knocking around the wildest regions of Chile and Peru. In the course of his wanderings, he had many exciting and dramatic experiences. The Andes country in particular seemed to encourage the unearthly and the weird. But one adventure involving poltergeist manifestation stood out in his mind above all the others.

When he was twenty-seven, Jack's company sent him to a small village in central Peru. He was to take charge of the operation of a small but very rich copper mine. The name of the village was Jauja, located about eighty miles east of Lima in the Andes chain.

One day a French priest, Father Condé, with whom Jack had become acquainted, came to see him. Jack noted that the priest, usually calm and collected, appeared to be in quite a flustered state.

"What's the trouble, Father?" asked Jack.

"Ah, my friend," said the priest rather breathlessly, "I have something I must discuss with you. There's a very queer thing going on in the town."

A few days before, the priest told him, an Indian named Vasquez had begged him to come to his home. He wished him to exorcise some spirits that had taken possession of the place and were driving him and his poor family frantic. For over a week, it seemed, Vasquez and his household had been repeatedly struck by stones thrown by invisible hands— while they were all *inside* the house. Vasquez said that sometimes this happened during the day but more frequently at night, even though the doors were closed and the shutters bolted securely.

"I tell you," continued Father Condé, "Vasquez was exceptionally excited—almost hysterical. I couldn't doubt his word that something really disturbing was going on. So I went to his house, and it was just as he said. I saw the stones falling myself! I tried some of the rites to lay the ghost, but it did no good. I'm completely baffled. Maybe you'd like to go see for yourself."

The strange situation interested Jack very much, and he suggested they call on the Vasquez family together. Father Condé thought they should go immediately, so they set out for the house. On the way they met the mayor of the town, explained what was going on, and asked if he'd like to go with them. The mayor agreed to go.

The three men went directly to the Vasquez house, a one-story structure of adobe brick roofed over with rough tile. Inside, the visitors found a combination living room and kitchen, a bedroom, and a storeroom.

Jack and the others learned that the family consisted of Vasquez, his wife, and three girls, whose ages ranged from eight to fifteen years. Vasquez's wife was in a hysterical condition. Her face and hands were covered with bruises and bumps, and the girls also had many bruises.

The family showed the three men a pile of rocks, ranging in size from pebbles to cobblestones, and there were also pieces of broken tile and lumps of hard, dried mud. All of these, said the mother, had been hurled at them during the past ten days. Curiously, none of the objects had struck Vasquez himself. Furthermore, no member of the family had been hit while *outside* the house.

The men inspected the premises carefully. Then, deciding to try an experiment, they took a chair from the living room and placed it in the middle of the nearly empty storeroom. Then the visitors persuaded one of the daughters to sit in it. This was the middle child, an intelligent-looking girl of about twelve. Her head and face were badly bruised and cut.

They then closed the heavy door leading to the living room and the three men—Jack, Father Condé, and the mayor— stood shoulder to shoulder in the doorway, with their backs against the door. Facing them was the girl in the center of the room. Behind her was a window with four small panes, set in a deep frame in the adobe wall. The window, which gave out onto the street, was nailed tightly shut. There was no other opening into the storeroom. Previously, the three had carefully examined the walls, ceiling, and hard mud floor. There was no place where anybody, or any large object, could possibly be concealed.

"We stood there, tense and expectant," Jack later recalled, "for quite a while. Nothing happened and after about twenty minutes our gaze, which had been fixed on the girl, may have wandered. I mention this to allow for any benefit of doubt about what happened.

"Suddenly, we heard a noise like a dull slap, followed by a thud. Then we saw, rolling across the floor, away from the girl, a stone about as large as a man's two fists. The stone had already struck the girl on the cheek with enough force to jerk her sideways, though not hard enough to knock her off the chair."

The girl burst into sobs, but remained seated on the chair. Jack and Father Condé remained where they were, but the mayor, in great excitement, rushed over to the stone and picked it up.

"This cannot be!" he shouted.

Keeping the heavy door closed, the three visitors went over the walls and ceiling of the room, inch by inch, trying to find a place where a stone might have been tossed through. But none was found.

"The girl," Jack subsequently related, "had been hit on the cheek, so the stone would have had to come from one side of the room. All three of us could have sworn that there had been no stones on the floor, and if that girl had had it concealed on her person she would have had to be a sleight-of-hand artist."

Jack also emphasized that from the sound of the thud and the effect of the blow, it appeared to have been thrown underhand from a distance of about six feet. Therefore, it could not possibly have come from the ceiling or from either the window or the door—even if those had been open. The three investigator/visitors were completely perplexed.

They also saw—with deep pity—that the little Vasquez girl's cheek was beginning to swell and they did what they could to soothe her. While Father Condé and the mayor of

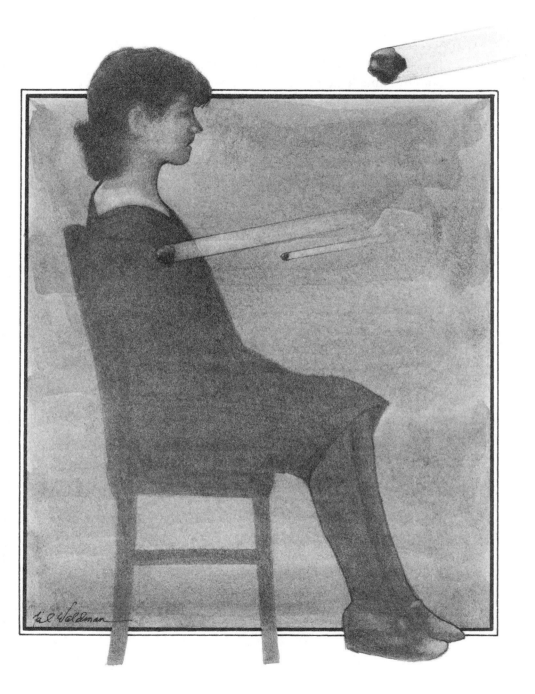

Jauja remained with the shaken family, Jack went out and bought some little presents for the Vasquez girls and some beer for the father and mother. When the three men left them, the family was at least as happy as it could be under the strange circumstances.

Jack Baragwanath continued to follow the case carefully. The strange stone attacks kept up for about a week more, then ceased as suddenly as they had commenced. For years, the young mining engineer tried to figure out some explanation for the odd events. But by his own admission, he never could.

THE DANCING
POLTERGEIST

ONE OF THE BEST-KNOWN CASES OF POLTERGEIST ACTIVITY
in Russia began in November 1870. It was unique in two
respects. First, the poltergeist did not manifest itself with
the usual flying crockery, stones, or other objects; rather, it
took the form of audible dancing steps. Second, in its final
manifestation, the poltergeist actually took on incendiary
abilities.

A wealthy landowner named Gregor Schapoff had been
away from his large country estate near Orensburg in
Uralsk province on a business trip. When he got back on
November 16, he discovered his whole household in a tur-
moil over what was apparently a ghost who danced. Two

days before, said his young wife Helena, their infant daughter had cried incessantly and refused to go to sleep. She then asked their cook, Maria, to entertain the baby until she fell asleep. Accordingly, Maria took her harmonica to the child's room and began to play for the little girl. Meanwhile, Helena had gone on chatting in the living room with her friend, the local miller's wife.

"Maria's very good with children," Helena had remarked to her friend. "If her harmonica playing doesn't put the little one to sleep, she dances for her. That always does the trick." After a few minutes, the two women heard Maria dancing a brisk three-step dance for the child.

Soon afterward, Maria had entered the living room and announced that the baby was fast asleep. Mrs. Schapoff had thanked the cook and dismissed her. Maria then told her mistress that she was going right to bed and retired to her quarters in the rear of the house.

Helena and the miller's wife had not been chatting for long when suddenly they heard a wild disturbance in the attic above their heads. The two women had stared at each other, mystified by the odd sounds. At first they were flurries of insane rappings with no discernible beat or rhythm to them. But then they had slowed and become measured and rhythmic. Finally they sounded exactly like the three-step dance that Maria had just performed for the child.

"Can that be Maria up there?" Helena had said. "It sounds just like her dancing."

"I don't see how," the miller's wife had replied. "We would have seen her pass by us to get there."

Helena told Gregor that she and her friend had walked out of the living room and back to the cook's quarters. Opening the door quietly, they had seen Maria sound asleep in her bed.

"That settles it," Helena had muttered in a frightened voice. "We've got to see who's up in the attic."

The dancing sounds had not stopped. It had taken will power for the terrified women to make their way up the stairs to the attic. Helena had a lantern with her, and they searched the attic, but they found no one up there. Still the dancing noises could be heard. Although the two women had made a hasty retreat downstairs, the rapping noises of the dancing appeared to race ahead of them, shaking the walls and rattling the windows. The miller's wife had then rushed off to fetch her husband and the gardener, while Helena went to see if her baby was all right.

When the miller's wife returned with her husband and the gardener, the loud dancing sounds had increased in intensity. So loud had they become that Helena's mother and mother-in-law, and Maria too, had awakened. Although the miller and the gardener searched the house and grounds thoroughly, they had found nothing. Yet the dancing sounds persisted until daybreak.

The following evening around ten o'clock, the dancing ghost once again began its rendition of the three-step. Although the house and estate were patrolled by servants and by neighbors who had heard of the strange goings-on, the invisible ghost danced on once more until daybreak.

After Gregor had heard all this, he shook his head in disbelief. He asked his wife whether she had been drinking his vodka and just imagined the whole wild tale. No, protested his wife, she had had nothing to drink. A practical, down-to-earth man, Gregor took little stock in stories of the supernatural. What he could not touch or see, he simply did not believe. Turning to his mother and mother-in-law, he demanded to know whether they verified the tale told by his wife.

"It's true, Gregor," affirmed his mother. "Something supernatural has come to this house."

The landowner shrugged and frowned, then made a remark about women concocting crazy stories that could only frighten servants and keep them from their tasks. Then he dispatched Maria to get the miller, whom he regarded as a very sensible and reliable person. When he arrived, Gregor asked him to substantiate the women's tale of the dancing ghost. The miller did so, saying it was correct in all details. However, he added, a couple of days ago he had removed a pigeon's nest from under one of the eaves of the house. Maybe the troublesome bird had returned, gotten into the house somehow, and was responsible for the odd noises everyone was hearing.

Delighted at this explanation, the stubborn Schapoff clapped the miller on the back and grinned broadly. "Naturally!" he exclaimed. "That is doubtless the cause of all this nonsense."

Feeling safer now that the landowner had returned, the whole household went to bed early. They were exhausted from the weird experiences of the past two days. Saying good night, Gregor stayed downstairs and decided to read for awhile before turning in. At a little past ten o'clock, however, he was distracted by some scratching noises above him. That, he thought, was probably the pigeon come back to the house, roaming around somewhere upstairs. But a few seconds later, as he listened closely, the noises changed into regular beats and taps, as if someone were dancing the three-step.

Thinking it must be his young wife having a bit of fun with him, Gregor put his book aside and went upstairs to Helena's room. He paused a few moments before her door to be sure that this was the source of the dancing sounds. It was and he resolved to give his wife a good talking-to. But when he slowly opened the door, the dancing sounds stopped immediately, and he saw that Helena was in her bed sleeping soundly, even snoring a little.

Mystified, Gregor was just shutting the door again when he heard multiple rappings coming from somewhere above Helena's bed. He tiptoed over to the bedstead and cocked one ear to the adjacent wall to listen more carefully to the sounds. Just as he did so, there came a deafening rap from the wall that nearly ruptured his eardrum. It also woke his wife, who sat straight up in bed, her lips pursed in a near scream. But she calmed down when she saw her husband.

"Gregor, what was that?" she exclaimed. "Did you hear it?"

"I didn't hear a thing," he lied, not wishing to upset his wife. Then, as if to punish him for the lie, came two thundering knocks that resounded through the whole house.

"I've had enough of this crazy business," declared Gregor angrily. "I've got to stop it." With that he put on his coat and grabbed a gun from a drawer. Downstairs he told some of the frightened servants to follow him, got out his watchdogs, and searched thoroughly about the house and grounds. Search as he would, the frustrated landowner could find no mischievous prankster on whom to blame the disturbances. But a curious thing about the dancing sounds, which still continued, was noticed by all that night. To those searching outside the house, the loud tappings appeared to be coming from inside. Yet to those who remained inside, it sounded as if someone were trying to batter the house down from without. Thwarted in his efforts to find the source of the sounds, Gregor finally called off the search in disgust.

The next night, after a fruitless all-day combing of the grounds, Schapoff decided to invite some of his neighbors in

to bear witness to the ghost. Promptly at ten o'clock—the
time when the disturbances usually began—the invisible
dancer began to perform. All night long it danced the familiar three-step; then, for a finale, it delivered such an explo-
sive blow to a door that it was half torn from its hinges.

By the following night, Gregor himself had become convinced that something supernatural had invaded his house.
Dreading the approach of ten o'clock, he paced around rest-
lessly until that hour arrived. But on this night the landowner and his family were amazed to hear nothing at all—no
scratchings, taps, or invisible feet dancing the three-step! It
appeared that peace had come once again to the Schapoff
country estate and the poltergeist had departed.

Four weeks later, just before Christmas, Gregor and his
wife were entertaining guests and the subject of the recent
disturbances came up. The guests were skeptical that such
phenomena were possible. Annoyed, Gregor then tempted
fate and called on Maria the cook to perform her three-step
dance. Probably all the ghost needed, he told his guests, was
a little coaxing to reappear again. Ignoring Helena's entreat-
ies not to go through with this, Gregor motioned for Maria
to begin dancing. She did so briskly. Almost immediately
afterward, a flurry of rappings was heard at the windows.
Then, as the guests listened in disbelief, they heard a perfect
repetition of the cook's dance coming from the attic.

"Ah," one guest accused the landowner, "you've got
someone else up there doing the dancing." However, when
Schapoff and some of the guests explored the attic, there
was no one there.

Again, at a New Year's Eve party, Gregor ordered Maria to
do her three-step dance to induce the invisible dancing ghost
to come forth. Cramming the house were many guests and,
after Maria stopped, they heard the repetitive echoes of her

three-step from the ceiling above them. On this occasion, the poltergeist was not content merely to put on its dancing act. It became so spirited and animated that it made some crude attempts at vocalizing snatches of Russian folk songs.

As a result of these two holiday parties, stories began to spread about the queer happenings at the Schapoffs' country mansion. In time, both scientists and spiritualists came to seek an audience with the dancing ghost. Some tried to communicate with it by a series of knocks but were unsuccessful. At length, word of these goings-on reached the Governor of Uralsk Province, who appointed a small committee of scientists to investigate the matter. This body eventually came to the conclusion that Helena Schapoff was producing the disturbances by some sort of trickery. A sharply worded letter of warning was dispatched to Gregor not to let the phenomena continue.

Yet they did continue and with a vengeance. Content before with merely rapping and dancing the three-step, the poltergeist now commenced its incendiary manifestations. It was Helena who was always at the center of these attacks. Balls of fire were seen to circle the house, and they often bounced against the windows of her room, as if seeking to enter and do her harm. Several times dresses in her closets burst into flame, and servants had to pour water on them. Once her mattress began burning from underneath.

The climax to these fiery events came one day when Helena was chatting with the miller and a house guest. All heard a crackling noise that seemed to come from under the floor of the living room. This was followed by a long, shrill howling sound. Then a blue spark appeared to pop up from the floor at Helena and immediately her thin dress caught fire. Before the horrified men, she became a virtual pillar of fire. Screaming in terror, she collapsed in a dead faint. With great courage and presence of mind, the house guest soon had the flames out, beating at them with his bare hands. The strange thing was that the guest suffered severe burns on his hands and arms, while Helena sustained not even a blister, though her dress was almost completely consumed by the flames.

At this point, the Schapoffs had had their fill of the dancing ghost—which had now become a dangerous menace that could deal out fiery destruction. Gregor closed up his country residence and moved into a town house in Iletski. From that time on the disturbances ceased, and Helena, whose health had grown steadily worse due to the poltergeist's onslaughts, recovered quickly. Unfortunately, the young woman died eight years later in childbirth.

Psychic researchers have continued to speculate about this unusual poltergeist case to the present day. They all agree that the person of Helena Schapoff seemed to offer the poltergeist its center of energy. Although poltergeist activity normally focuses around children and teenagers, Helena was not far from being a teenager herself. She was only twenty when the manifestations began. Some experts have theorized that some psychic shock, perhaps in her marriage, had liberated a powerful psychokinetic (PK) energy from her main personality, so that subconsciously she herself willed the phenomena. Or perhaps, other researchers have theorized, a psychic residue of energy in the Schapoff mansion— perhaps built up there by a former resident—had found a sympathetic energy source in young Helena's psyche, or soul. This theory of poltergeist activity holds that a focus of bottled up energy in the psychic atmosphere can release itself violently when a person with the right telepathic affinity comes on the scene to trigger it. If so, Helena seems to have been that person.

THE HAUNTED SHORES
OF SANDWOOD BAY

SITUATED AT THE EXTREME NORTHWESTERN TIP OF THE Scottish mainland, Cape Wrath is well named. In spite of its desolate beauty, the Cape is incessantly lashed by frantic seas, and its rockbound coast is littered with the skeletons of wrecked ships that dared brave the Atlantic in those northern latitudes.

One bleak isolated beach on Cape Wrath is known as Sandwood Bay. There, one fall afternoon in the 1930s, a Scots tenant farmer and his son ventured farther than usual from their fields in search of firewood. The two spoke little as they roamed along the beach, gathering wood from the wrecks on the utterly deserted Sandwood Bay dunes. So far had they wandered with their small pony that they found themselves in this strange region—and did not know that the beach on which they were working was thought to be haunted. The inhabitants of nearby Durness and other villages were accustomed to visitors coming back from Sandwood Beach with scary tales of an apparition and odd happenings, both on the beach and around some of its deserted cottages.

Interrupting his wood-gathering, the son glanced over the western horizon at the declining sun. "Father," he began, "night's coming. We'd best be heading home now."

The older man also raised his eyes to the sun. "Aye, we'll be on our way now, lad."

Just then the little pony neighed skittishly. The two men whirled around to see what had disturbed the animal and were abruptly aware that a man was confronting them not far away.

"Evening, sir," stammered the startled farmer. "We did nae see ye standin' there."

The stranger appeared to be a seaman of some sort. A short bearded man, he wore sea boots, an officer's peaked cap, and a dark blue jacket with brass buttons. These articles of clothing, the two farmers later recalled, looked like those that a mariner of the previous century might have worn. The stranger stared at them and then yelled in a hollow, cavernous voice, "My property! This is my property, do you understand? Drop it and leave this place!"

Astonished and filled with terror, the farmer and his son promptly dumped all the wood they had accumulated and, grabbing the pony's reins, fled the beach for home.

A few years later on a sunny summer afternoon, the same stocky seafaring figure was seen by the members of a large fishing party. These witnesses noticed particularly that the figure was wearing a peaked mariner's cap and a dark blue jacket. The latter was adorned with brass buttons that glinted in the sun's rays. The members of the fishing party first saw the figure standing next to a sandy mound; next, they saw it walk slowly along the crest of a dune and then vanish behind a hillock.

Thinking that the man might be a poacher, the leader of the fishing party dispatched a servant across the beach to investigate. Several minutes later, the servant returned. Shaken and whitefaced, he reported that he had seen no one at all. Moreover, he could find no footprints in the sand at the spot where they had all seen the sailor.

Still standing today high atop the ridge facing Cape Wrath Lighthouse, amid heather and bracken about a mile from the dunes of Sandwood Bay, are the remains of Sandwood Cottage. Untenanted for over four decades, it is probably the most remote and solitary dwelling on the Scottish mainland. No road, not even a trail, leads to it.

Here, in the early 1960s, an old fisherman named Angus Morrison, unwilling to continue his long journey home after dark, spent a night in the cottage. Just as he was about to fall asleep in one of the dusty bedrooms, Angus heard footsteps outside and then a loud tapping at the front window.

Dressing quickly, the old fisherman descended to the ground floor to investigate. Louder and louder grew the tapping noises. Glancing toward the window, Angus clearly saw the bearded face of a sailor looking into the cottage; he wore a jacket with brass buttons and a peaked officer's cap. Yet when the fisherman went outside and looked about Sandwood Cottage and the nearby beach, he could see no one. He also looked for footprints, but found none except his own.

On a similar occasion some months later, Angus again spent the night at the deserted cottage. While he did not see the seafaring man this time, he was awakened during the night by weird thumping noises. He also had the strange feeling that he was being suffocated by a dense, hateful atmosphere pressing down upon his body. Another local

man, a shepherd named Sandy Gunn, also had occasion to pass a night in Sandwood Cottage. He told some friends that he had clearly heard ghostly shuffling footsteps downstairs. Searching the entire house, Sandy reported that he had found nothing out of the ordinary.

In the late 1960s, two Englishmen spent the night in Sandwood Cottage. They felt too weary to continue their long hike that evening and planned to go on next morning to Kinlochbervie where they could catch a bus to Lairg. In the early morning hours, they were awakened by thudding noises, and soon the whole cottage began to shudder with thunderous bangings and crashes. Unlike Morrison and Gunn, the two men were sleeping downstairs, and the sounds seemed to issue from the empty rooms above them. Terrified, they listened to doors being flung open and slammed shut again, windows being smashed, and ponderous tramping footsteps loud enough to have been made by a horse. The following day in Kinlochbervie the Englishmen confided to the postmaster that no sum of money could ever persuade them to spend another night in Sandwood Cottage.

Curious tourists still make expeditions to the haunted beach that rings bleakly beautiful Sandwood Bay. And once in awhile, roaming among the wrecked ships and ghostly sand dunes, some tell of glimpsing a strange stocky seafaring man wearing a peaked officer's cap and a brass-buttoned jacket.

In this curious apparition case, it may have been—and perhaps still is—the earthbound spirit body of a once-living man lingering about this area for some reason. Perhaps the sailor's ship was wrecked offshore and he was drowned. Or maybe, judging from what he said to the farmer and his son, he once owned property on Sandwood Bay and still, long after his death, resents the intrusion of living persons on it.

"DEAD" VOICES FROM A HAUNTED TAPE RECORDER

ONE DAY EARLY IN APRIL 1960, A BURLY AND WELL-KNOWN Swedish painter named Friedrich Jurgenson entered one of Stockholm's leading electronics stores. It was midday, lunchtime was fast approaching, and Mr. Jurgenson asked one of the sales clerks if he could talk to the store's manager. The 60-year-old artist had brought with him a tape recorder that had been performing in a strange manner, and he wished to have it checked over for mechanical accuracy. He had purchased the device at this same electronics store some weeks before.

The painter had undergone something of a struggle with himself in deciding to return the tape recorder for examination. Being an artist of some reputation, he did not want to be labeled as some kind of eccentric or "nut," especially because in a few days he would be holding a one-man exhibition of his work in one of Stockholm's foremost galleries. Still, he had made the decision and here he was.

"The manager will see you now, sir," the sales clerk told him.

Mr. Jurgenson stepped into the manager's office and put his tape recorder on the man's desk.

"Is something defective with the machine?" the manager asked.

"That's what I'd like to find out," Jurgenson replied. "Actually, I have no specific complaint about its performance. In fact, it seems to be working well. Nevertheless, I'd like you to make a complete inspection of it, down to every internal connection. Whatever this costs, I'll gladly pay it. I'll be back in a week to see if you've found anything wrong with the machine."

What was it about the recorder's behavior that had upset the artist so? It was this: a few weeks before, he had discovered that the machine was apparently acting as a link between the living and the dead! He had bought the recorder in order to make notes and suggestions to himself about his paintings as they entered his mind—and before he forgot them. At his studio in the suburbs of Stockholm, the artist had set up the machine so that it would be ready to use when he needed it.

One night not long after this, Jurgenson conceived some ideas about a portrait he was painting. Here was his chance to use his new machine. He switched the tape recorder on and started to dictate his thoughts into the hand-held microphone. Then he rewound the tape and started to play it back. He was dumbfounded to hear a harsh, discordant jumble of sounds interrupting his own speaking voice.

Jurgenson naturally thought that the tape must be defective. So he selected a new one and ran it through the recorder to make sure that it was clear of any random recording noise. Rewinding it, he once again dictated his thoughts concerning the portrait. And again he was startled by a cacophony of sounds interfering with his own voice.

This time, however, the artist was amazed to hear, through the confused jumble of sounds, several coherent voices emerging. Soon they broke out in a weird chant that echoed throughout his studio: "We live! We live! We are not dead!" Then the voices slowly faded out and abruptly vanished. On rolled the tape, silent now.

Jurgenson then decided that his ears must be playing tricks on him. He rewound the tape and played it again. There were the same voices, faithfully recorded, and speaking to him again. In the days that followed, the painter made frequent use of the recorder—and each time the mystifying intruders broke in on his recorded thoughts with their pleading supplications.

Subsequently the artist tried everything he could think of to rule out natural explanations for the occurrences. He purchased several new tapes, but the phenomena still persisted. Gifted painter though he was, he was not a man who possessed mechanical aptitude; he once confided to a friend that he could not even repair a simple electrical fuse. Nevertheless, following the wiring diagram in his instruction book, he checked as best he could the components and circuitry of the machine. As far as he could see, everything appeared to be in order. It was at this point that he decided to take the recorder back to the shop for a thorough examination.

When Jurgenson returned to the electronics store to pick up his machine, he was assured by the manager that it was in perfect working order. Jurgenson then began to tell his story; since he was something of a celebrity, the newspapers picked it up and soon it was public knowledge. His tape recorder was somehow able to pick up the voices of deceased persons! Electronics experts and skeptics were quick to remind everyone that tape recorders were ideal for playing hoaxes. Audio tapes, they said, could easily be doctored and faked in all kinds of ways.

As for Jurgenson, he had not bargained for all this publicity, and he was confused and disturbed. Certainly he had not wanted to create a cheap advertising stunt for the sake of his upcoming exhibition. To show his sincerity he invited anyone who wished—scientists, engineers, psychic investigators— to examine his tape recorder and listen to the voices for themselves.

As the strange occurrences gained more publicity, electronics enthusiasts and others came regularly to Jurgenson's studio. They combed his rooms for concealed equipment, monitored his recording sessions, and meticulously checked his recorder and tapes. None of them succeeded in finding trickery or fraud of any kind.

Fascinated with the phenomena, Jurgenson continued with his recording. One day late in August, with ten witnesses in his studio, he picked up something very odd. It was a voice delivering a prolonged harangue in German. One of those present, a German technician, suddenly straightened up and exclaimed, "That's Hitler's voice!"

"But," objected another listener, "Hitler's been dead for over fifteen years."

Yet apparently it was true. Some recordings in a local radio station made during World War II of the Fuehrer's voice were checked against the voice on Jurgenson's tape. The speech elements matched perfectly. The voice on the artist's

tape seemed to be speaking to someone in a concentration camp. It was expressing abject remorse for the atrocities committed during World War II.

As the months passed, people ceased to make fun of Jurgenson and his strange tape recordings. Reporters formed the habit of visiting his studio from time to time to write up the latest eerie message recorded by his machine. And Jurgenson rarely turned them away or failed to provide them with good "copy."

Once Eva Braun, Hitler's mistress, came through on the tape recorder. In a shrill whisper, she told of her last-minute marriage to Hitler in the Berlin bunker just before their suicides, and their final hours together. Over the next few years, Jurgenson recorded scores of tapes containing over 150 voices that could be definitely identified. Among them were those of David Lloyd George, the Emperor Napoleon, Prince Otto von Bismarck, and the executed American murderer, Caryl Chessman.

The Swedish artist never attempted any scientific explanation of the phenomena. Evidently, he often said, his recording device had been chosen by forces beyond his comprehension to act as a receiving station for persons no longer living on the earth plane. And as he continued to record the "dead" voices, he came to believe that these personalities did live on in some other, happier dimension.

THE NEWARK POLTERGEIST

THE DISTURBANCES THAT BEGAN ON MAY 6, 1961, AT THE home of Mrs. Maybelle Clark in Newark, New Jersey, lasted only a bare two weeks. But the case has proved to be one of the best documented of poltergeist activity in recent years.

The "focus person" was Mrs. Clark's grandson, a 13-year-old youth who at the time was living with his grandmother in her first-floor four-room apartment on Rose Street. The boy's name was Ernest Rivers, and the first event occurred on his thirteenth birthday. As Ernest was doing his homework that evening, he was amazed to see a pepper shaker come floating through the air and land gently beside him. This was the start of an almost-daily barrage of flying objects, mostly crockery and glassware.

When the first of the phenomena occurred, Mrs. Clark told only family members and a few of her best friends about them. But some of these persons eventually told others, and before long word of the disturbances had leaked out. When newspaper reporters began to appear to cover the "ghost story," she was reticent with them and refused to allow them to photograph her or Ernest. Mrs. Clark was understandably worried for two reasons. First, she didn't want people to think she and her grandson were crazy and "seeing things that weren't there." Second, she was afraid she might be evicted from her apartment. Mrs. Clark had lived in this housing development for twenty years, and she did not want the housing authority to think she was an undesirable tenant or involved in some mischievous prank.

One of the first persons to investigate the case was Irving Laskowitz, director of tenant relations of the Newark Housing Authority. After he had looked around the apartment and questioned the boy and his grandmother, he concluded: "We found no evidence of manual participation. I only wish we had; naughty children are much easier to deal with than invisible pranksters."

Laskowitz then suggested that Mrs. Clark and Ernest move to a different apartment in the building. Perhaps this would end the phenomena. But Mrs. Clark bravely refused.

"No," she said firmly. "I don't think this is going to go on for ever."

"Well," Laskowitz replied with some humor, "pretty soon you'll run out of things to break."

And indeed, as the days passed, Mrs. Clark's supply of crockery and glassware was fast becoming depleted. One evening as she and Ernest were eating in the kitchen, four cups rose out of a punch bowl in the living room, sailed into the kitchen, and smashed on the floor. At other times, a drinking glass became airborne from the kitchen sink, turned a corner, and shattered on the living room floor; a cup

was seen to glide across the pantry shelf and smash on the kitchen floor; an ashtray hopped over a Bible on a table and landed on the carpet below; a light bulb became unscrewed from a floor lamp in Ernest's bedroom and shattered; a bottle of disinfectant toppled from the bathroom shelf and smashed to pieces on the tile floor; and once a small mirror in Ernest's bedroom fell and was cracked.

By this time news of the disturbances had aroused the neighborhood, and Mrs. Clark's tenant friends—eager to help or just to witness the antics of the "ghost" for themselves—showed up frequently at the apartment. Often Mrs. Clark, frightened and glad to have company, let them in. In this way several people were able to confirm that something unusual was definitely going on. One of these, Mrs. Cordelia Holland, who lived on the third floor of the complex, stated: "We were in the kitchen and suddenly I saw this glass decanter on top of the refrigerator start to move toward the edge. I yelled and caught it just in time. I put it back and made sure it was in the middle of the refrigerator top. A half hour later, when we weren't looking, we heard a crash and found the decanter on the floor."

Another time Mrs. Clark, Ernest, and two women friends were having coffee in the kitchen. Suddenly they were amazed to see a jar of Vaseline, known to have been on the bathroom shelf, come whizzing through the pantry area, veer around a corner, and land with a thud on the living room rug. One morning Mrs. Clark was awakened by harsh scraping noises. She saw a bottle of furniture polish inching along her bedroom floor all by itself. As the days went by, Mrs. Clark's initial fear almost left her. It was replaced by anger at having to clean up the contents of smashed bottles and pick up the broken glass.

On the sixth day of the occurrences, a heavy electric steam

iron rose from its position on a storage shelf in the hall and sailed into Mrs. Clark's bedroom. Its cord was trailing straight out behind it like the tail of a kite. The amazed Mrs. Clark watched as it came to rest on the floor. She later remarked that she never would have believed her eyes had she been alone—but she wasn't. Mrs. Holland was sitting with her in the bedroom and saw it, too.

A few days later, James Moore, a Newark Housing Authority executive, and Ward Ulrich, a *Newark Star-Ledger* reporter, were both in the Clark apartment. Ulrich was standing in a hallway when he heard someone give a low wail; he whirled around just in time to see a bottle zip through the air and land in Mrs. Clark's bedroom. Ulrich picked it up and both men saw that it was a medicine bottle with a plastic cap. It had been resting on one of the hall shelves before it became airborne. During this event, Ernest was seen to be standing just inside his own room. Later Ulrich said he doubted that the boy could have thrown the bottle from where he was standing.

Ulrich closely questioned Mrs. Clark, Ernest, and other witnesses about the odd events. They were all convinced that what they had seen were real happenings and that no trickery was involved. "These witnesses," Ulrich said, "were all rational and normally intelligent people. None of them seemed emotional or hysterical."

Actually, far greater hysteria was shown by the crowds who often gathered outside the apartment building, eager to get a look at the "ghost house." Frequently there were drunken adults and noisy children among them. In time, Mrs. Clark and Ernest grew more frightened of them than of the "spooks" in their apartment. On some nights the boy and his grandmother sought escape from the poltergeist at the home of Mrs. Clark's daughter and her husband, Ruth and

William Hargwood. At such times, no poltergeist activity occurred.

By this time, psychical researchers had become interested in the case and, when interviewed by reporters, the theory of emotionally upset youngsters possibly causing the disturbances came to the fore. Naturally this caused suspicion to fall on young Ernest. One paper began calling him "the boy who makes things fly." In Ernest's case, there were good grounds for the theory, for in his young life the boy had suffered a great deal of unhappiness and emotional upset.

In 1956 Ernest's mother, Ann Clark Rivers, had killed his father, a professional boxer. During her trial she testified that on that night she had dreamed her husband was going to kill her with a gun he kept in the bedroom. Badly frightened, and before she was fully awake, Ann Rivers had obtained the gun and killed her husband. She pleaded guilty to a charge of manslaughter in the second degree and was sentenced to from 18 to 22 years in a minimum security reformatory for women. After this, Ernest was sent to live with his grandparents in the Newark apartment house. Then, in 1960, his grandfather died. The following year, in April, he and his grandmother learned that Ernest's mother had escaped from the reformatory. Although she was later apprehended and returned, Ann Rivers was still at large when the poltergeist activity took place in Mrs. Clark's Newark apartment. If the disturbed-teenager theory is correct, it is likely that Ann Rivers' escape triggered Ernest's intense emotional state and perhaps set the stage for the disturbances that occurred a month later.

In any case, by mid-May Mrs. Clark's apartment was besieged by well-meaning visitors who wanted to investigate the phenomena, help in any way they could, or catch a glimpse of "that boy who makes things fly." Two Rutgers

University researchers arrived who wanted to test Ernest for PK ability, but Mrs. Clark refused the offer. Another man came who had had years of experience in exorcising poltergeists. Despite his efforts, he failed, for that same night two more events took place. A bottle of antiseptic flew out of the bathroom medicine cabinet and landed in Mrs. Clark's bedroom. Then a can of paint on a shelf in the hall was flung to the floor.

At this point, a New York University professor of psychology named Dr. Charles Wrege entered the picture. Dr. Wrege had long been interested in poltergeist events, and he visited the Clark apartment a number of times. He quickly gained the confidence of Mrs. Clark and Ernest. On three separate occasions while in the apartment with Ernest, Dr. Wrege saw objects in flight propelled by an unseen force. But he declared that the boy was not standing in the right places to have thrown the objects. Wrege measured distances and checked every object in the rooms to make sure no pranks were being played. Soon he was convinced that Ernest had done nothing overtly physical to move the objects.

Then came the evening of May 13. Outside the apartment the crowd of people were especially restless and noisy. Once in awhile someone would knock loudly on the door and demand to see "the boy that makes things fly." Around 10 o'clock William Hargwood showed up to take his mother-in-law and Ernest home with him. That was when those present saw a glass ashtray snap in two with a loud report. Seeing this, Mrs. Clark put in a quick call to Dr. Wrege, because she'd promised to let him know of the next poltergeist event. When the professor arrived, he saw that Ernest and his grandmother were going to leave with William Hargwood.

"Couldn't you leave the boy here with me?" he requested.

"Maybe there'll be other manifestations when we're alone in the apartment together."

The frightened Mrs. Clark finally agreed to this and left with her son-in-law. Ernest and the professor settled down to see what—if anything—would occur next. Their wait was a short one. Both were in the kitchen when they heard a loud crash in the living room. In they dashed to find a table lamp hurled to the floor. Wrege was sure Ernest hadn't over-turned the lamp because the boy had been right next to him in the kitchen. Even so, he checked the smashed lamp and its plug and cord to see whether any strings or other apparatus had been rigged up to pull it over. But he turned up nothing.

About ten minutes after this event, Ernest and Wrege were back in the kitchen standing a few feet away from the drainboard on the sink. Suddenly a glass standing on the board rose into the air and dashed to fragments on the floor. The curious thing about this event was that they both saw the glass shatter *before* it hit the floor.

Next, Dr. Wrege and Ernest heard a crash and the sound of breaking glass from Mrs. Clark's bedroom. Here they found that a perfectly natural physical event had taken place. Someone in the milling, noisy crowd outside had flung a rock through the window. By now Ernest was nearly frightened out of his wits—not so much by the poltergeist activity as by the dangerous, ugly mob outside. At this point Dr. Wrege phoned the police and William Hargwood, who arrived in short order. The police took a look around the apartment to try to find out what was causing the strange events, but could find nothing amiss. They then dispersed the crowd of people outside and left.

As the two men and the boy were getting ready to leave the apartment, a pepper shaker suddenly hit Ernest's Uncle William on the back, then fell to the floor. Seconds later a glass ashtray grazed his chin. Hargwood was not in the least hurt by these blows, however. The ashtray was replaced on a table but a minute later it fell of its own accord directly between the two men. Later Dr. Wrege admitted that at this time he did not have the boy under close observation, but his belief was that Ernest did not throw these objects or try to displace them.

The next event turned out to be the final one of the case. Thoroughly scared by now, Ernest was standing in the hallway ready to leave through the front door. Wrege and Hargwood were still in the living room. At this time, Dr. Wrege saw a salt shaker come sailing in from the kitchen, which was opposite the hall where Ernest was waiting at the front door. It struck Hargwood on the head—again, surprisingly, he was not hurt by the blow. This time Dr. Wrege could say with certainty that the boy could not possibly have thrown the object.

In any case, Wrege, Ernest, and his Uncle William lost no time in escaping to the Hargwood home. For some weeks the boy stayed with his uncle and aunt. When he finally did return to the apartment to live with his grandmother, the poltergeist activity did not resume.

So ended the Newark poltergeist affair. The case is particularly noteworthy because it was the first to be reported from a housing development. The activity, which consisted of over fifty separate events, centered around one small apartment in a large building complex. That Ernest was the "focus person" cannot be doubted, for there was never any poltergeist activity when he was not present in the apartment. And in all probability, if the PK theory is correct, the objects involved were made to move by the psychokinetic energy unconsciously released by the emotionally upset adolescent boy.

"POPPER," THE LONG ISLAND POLTERGEIST

NOT MANY CHILDREN HAVE BEEN WELCOMED HOME FROM school with a five-gun salute, but when the Herrmann children, twelve-year-old James Jr. and thirteen-year-old Lucille, walked in the front door of their Long Island, New York, home at 3:30 on the afternoon of February 3, 1958, things began going crazy. It was here in this quiet suburban home that one of the best-known of all poltergeist cases took place. The disturbances lasted a little over a month and, as tabulated by parapsychologists, consisted of sixty-seven separate, documented events.

When the children returned home from school that afternoon, Jimmy went upstairs to his room and found that a ceramic doll and a ship model of his had been smashed.

Baffled, the boy reported this damage to his mother, who then looked around in other rooms to see if anything else had been disturbed. On her own dresser she discovered that a bottle of Holy Water had been knocked over (the Herrmanns were Roman Catholics); its cap was unscrewed and the water was dripping down on the floor.

At this point, no noises had been heard. But during the next forty-five minutes, a series of poppings was heard in various parts of the house. The loud noises sounded like so many bottles of champagne being uncorked. Scurrying from room to room, Mrs. Herrmann and her two children found that the caps to numerous bottles—most of which contained cosmetics, soft drinks, and cleaning agents—had become unscrewed and the bottles were lying on their sides pouring out their contents. While Jimmy and his mother were in the cellar, they saw a half-gallon bottle of bleach rise from a cardboard box and come sailing toward them. It smashed almost at Mrs. Herrmann's feet. Jimmy had the presence of mind to pull some clothing on a clothesline in front of her so that she would be protected from the flying glass and splashing bleach.

When the disturbances had apparently ceased for the time being, an unnerved Mrs. Herrmann got on the phone to her husband, an Air France representative working in New York City. In a hushed voice she reported to James Herrmann, Sr., the loud popping noises, the unscrewed bottles, and the spilled liquids. Herrmann asked if anyone had been hurt. When his wife said no, Herrmann, though puzzled, saw no reason to leave work early. Later, on the commuter train, he pondered these odd explosions. He concluded that some chemical reaction must have taken place in the bottles nearly simultaneously, causing them all to pop open in a short space of time. Maybe, he speculated, some atmospheric condition in the house, such as excess humidity or the heating turned up too high, had triggered the explosions. But when he arrived home and inspected the burst bottles, he was thoroughly perplexed. All the bottles had screw-type caps that required several turns before they could be removed. If they had been simple crimped caps, such as those on soft-drink bottles, his theories might have been correct. At any rate, the family by now had composed themselves, and Herrmann decided to forget about the mystery.

But this was just the beginning of the weird events in the Herrmann household. Three days later, Lucille and Jimmy came home from school as usual and the popping noises were heard again. In the bathroom, two bottles of rubbing alcohol and one of nail polish were found minus their caps, tipped over, and spilling their contents. A wine bottle in the linen closet was overturned and gurgling its liquid out over sheets and towels. Again in the basement, a bottle of Clorox was seen to spring out of its box and smash on the cement floor.

The next night young Jimmy was the only person at home when the cap on an ammonia bottle under the kitchen sink became unscrewed and the liquid dumped all over. When his father learned of this, he began to suspect that perhaps his son was the cause of it all. Jimmy was a bright, imaginative boy who was much interested in science at school. It was entirely possible, Herrmann speculated, that the boy might be attempting to work out a series of bizarre experiments for the fun of it—at the expense of his family. He might even have figured out how to slip some chemical into the bottles before he went to school, so timing the poppings that they would occur later. Herrmann had a weekend coming up and he decided to spend it keeping tabs on Jimmy's activities.

No poppings occurred on Saturday, but Sunday, February 9, was a banner day at the Herrmanns' house. The father had been watching Jimmy closely, but by the time the whole family gathered in the living room a little after ten o'clock in the morning, Herrmann still had not seen the boy doing anything suspicious. Thus, he was surprised when odd noises were heard coming from various rooms. Checking through the house, they found another bottle of holy water uncapped and spilling in the parents' bedroom. A bottle of toilet water had fallen, having lost its screw cap and rubber stopper. In the bathroom, a bottle of shampoo and one of Kaopectate had been unscrewed, fallen over, and were emptying out their contents. In the cellar a can of paint thinner had opened and was spilling. Checking on all these events had taken about a quarter of an hour and it was now about ten thirty.

At this time, Herrmann noted, Jimmy had gone into the bathroom and was brushing his teeth. Still not convinced that his son was completely innocent, he confronted him at the doorway of the bathroom and began questioning him. Jimmy protested vigorously that he had had nothing to do with the bottle poppings. Between father and son on a Formica vanity table stood the same two bottles of shampoo and Kaopectate that had spilled a few minutes before; Mrs. Herrmann had put them there after she cleaned up the mess. Suddenly Herrmann and Jimmy were astonished to see both bottles begin to move—but in opposite directions. The shampoo toppled off the table and crashed on the tile floor. The Kaopectate simply slid along the vanity until it fell into the sink, before which Jimmy was standing.

It was this event, witnessed by himself and his son, that convinced James Herrmann that something unique was going on in his home.

"This is too much," he recalled saying later. "We've got troubles."

Herrmann went directly to the phone and called the Nassau County Police Department. The desk sergeant listened patiently to what sounded like a wild tale of bottles popping their caps and flying about rooms; in fact, he accused Herrmann of having been drinking. Herrmann protested he hadn't. The sergeant relented and said he would send an officer to investigate. Accordingly, Patrolman James Hughes soon arrived on the scene. He was sitting in the living room trying to absorb the strange stories the family was blurting out to him when a noise was heard in the bathroom. As it happened, Hughes had checked the bathroom upon his arrival and nothing had been amiss there. Once again Mrs. Herrmann had put all to rights, including the Kaopectate bottle on the vanity. Rushing into the bathroom, Hughes and the others saw that the Kaopectate container had been overturned. Hughes was certain he had seen it standing upright. "I can swear to that," he later wrote in his official report.

When Hughes reported back to Detective Joseph Tozzi, the latter listened skeptically. He strongly suspected that some person or persons were responsible for the happenings. In any event, he wanted to see for himself, so he took official charge of the case the following Tuesday, February 11. That afternoon when he, Mrs. Herrmann, Lucille, and Jimmy were in the house, an atomizer bottle of perfume on the teenaged girl's dresser was found tipped over, its cap off, and the scent spilled. A noise had been heard when this event occurred and Tozzi noted that nobody had been in the girl's room at the time. In the cellar, it was found that the paint thinner had again lost its cap and was spilled. The next day Tozzi had a serious talk with the Herrmann children; he frankly believed that one of them was responsible for the occurrences. But Jimmy and Lucille still claimed they had nothing to do with the strange events.

For the next few days, the poltergeist events were confined to mere overturnings of the holy water bottle in the parents' bedroom. But with a difference this time—the water was found to be quite warm to the touch. However, on the evening of February 15, the activity took a more exciting turn. While Mr. and Mrs. Herrmann were in other parts of the house, Lucille, Jimmy, and their Aunt Marie were watching television. Suddenly they saw a porcelain figurine on the coffee table rise up and begin to float through the air. Moments later it crashed down unbroken on the carpet. The strange thing was that, even though it hit a soft surface, it made an unusually loud noise.

More events took place the next Sunday. Mrs. Herrmann found her perfume bottle overturned and spilling on her dresser. Later, after the children had gone to bed, the parents heard a noise in Jimmy's bedroom. They found that a small plastic angel had been transported across his room to the dresser, where it knocked down a Davy Crockett doll and a ship model. A few minutes later, while Herrmann was on the phone reporting all this to Tozzi, he and his wife heard another loud noise from Jimmy's room. A globe of the world had been dashed to the floor. Several minutes later another crash was heard in Jimmy's room. They found the night table lamp on the floor with its bulb smashed.

This was enough for Herrmann. He picked up his terrified son, carried him into the master bedroom, and put him to bed there. But the transfer did little to check the poltergeist's antics. Half an hour later the night table in the master bedroom overturned with a loud crash. By this time it was becoming clear to everybody that the disturbances were centering around Jimmy, and both Tozzi and Herrmann once again began to suspect that the boy was in some mysterious way responsible for them.

Only two events occurred during the first part of the next week. On Monday morning, Mrs. Herrmann found the same porcelain figurine on the floor in the living room, two feet from the coffee table it had stood on. On Wednesday she heard a noise in the living room; again the figurine had fallen, as it had on Monday. All this while, Tozzi had been bending over backward to discover some physical cause for the happenings. Thinking they might be caused by high-frequency radio waves, Tozzi had his men question a resident in the area who was a "ham" radio operator. It turned out this man hadn't used his set in years. Tozzi then contacted the Long Island Lighting Company and an oscillograph was installed in the cellar of the Herrmann home to pick up any unusual vibrations. None were picked up, even while the occurrences were happening. The police lab in Mineola was given five of the bottles that had lost their caps for analysis; none was found to contain any foreign matter other than their normal contents. The lighting company was summoned again to examine the house's wiring, fuse panels, and ground cables for faulty electrical emissions. Everything was found to be in order.

Early on Thursday, February 20, a loud pop was heard in the basement. Lucille found another Clorox bottle had lost its cap and was spilling. At eight o'clock that same night, when the whole family—including Tozzi—was either in the dining room or basement, a very loud smashing noise was heard in the living room. A porcelain figure had left a table and hit the wooden desk about ten feet away; the impact had broken the figurine's arm and left a dent in the wood. Ninety minutes later, Jimmy, Lucille, Mrs. Herrmann, and Tozzi were in the dining room area when a sugar bowl on the dining room table suddenly took off and smashed close to Tozzi's feet. A few minutes after this, an ink bottle on the same table lost its screw cap and sailed toward the front door, then suddenly dropped and splashed ink on the floor. Two more incidents happened that same night. A figurine in the living room was found smashed against the desk and completely demolished. And a toy metal horse fell at Tozzi's feet while he and Jimmy were in the basement. At this point the frustrated Tozzi overreacted and subjected Jimmy to stern questioning, even accusing him of having thrown the toy horse. All the while the boy stoutly denied being the cause of any of the disturbances.

That same day, the meticulous Tozzi had checked all the electrical outlets, the TV, and the oil burner to see if they were possibly causing the phenomena. But they were all in good order. In addition, he looked at the water leaders, fuse boxes, and the electrical connections in the attic. Nothing seemed wrong with them. After the unnerving events of February 20, the Herrmanns decided to vacate the house for a couple of days and stay with relatives. Tozzi took this opportunity to spend a night alone in the house, but nothing at all of a supernatural nature occurred.

When the Herrmanns returned on Sunday afternoon, the poltergeist activity recommenced with a vengeance. About three o'clock a heavy cut glass centerpiece rose from the dining room table and landed on the bottom shelf of a cabinet several feet away. A little after eight in the evening, a figurine on the end table, the same one seen by Aunt Marie a few days before, was heard to smash against a desk that was a dozen feet away. A newspaper reporter from *Newsday* was present and witnessed this event. At eight thirty, when Mrs. Herrmann and the children were in their rooms, Mr. Herrmann and the reporter were rocked by a loud thud that shook the whole house. The heavy dresser in Jimmy's room had toppled over.

By this time, news of the baffling events in the Herrmann household had appeared in the papers and other media. To the Herrmanns, this unwanted publicity was, in its way, more of a nuisance than the strange events themselves. As the media gave the story more and more play, crackpot letters began to fill the family mailbox. Crude scrawls exhorted the Herrmanns to take heart against Satan; some even condemned them for having committed unprintable sins which were the cause of their trouble. Once or twice, self-styled preachers of obscure Gospel sects showed up and conducted rites of exorcism on the front lawn. In the meanwhile, disturbances at the house were still in full swing. On Monday afternoon, a terrific crash in Jimmy's room was heard and again the heavy dresser was found on its side. Lucille, in the basement at the time, remarked later, "It sounded like the walls were caving in!" In the newspapers and over radio and TV, the mysterious force had come to be called "Popper" because of the many bottle-popping incidents.

That same Monday night, more fireworks were scheduled by "Popper." At eight thirty, when no one was in the living room, a noise was heard there. A ceramic ashtray that had reposed on the coffee table was found shattered some four feet away. About thirty minutes later, Jimmy's globe of the world came bouncing out of his room, narrowly missing the reporter who was seated in the living room. Next, just a couple of minutes after James Herrmann returned home from work, a terrific blow was heard in Jimmy's room. Everyone rushed in and saw that the poltergeist had worked its mightiest feat to date: a heavy bookcase was found wedged upside down between the radiator and the bed. Later, a picture hanging over Jimmy's bed was discovered on the floor in the middle of the room.

The following morning, after Herrmann had left for work and while the children were dressing for school, a loud crash was heard and Mrs. Herrmann dashed into the hall. She called to the children. Both answered that it was not in their rooms. By this time the children had been sternly instructed not to move from where they were when some disturbance occurred. Then everyone went into the master bedroom and found that a sixteen-inch plaster figure of the Virgin Mary had left James Herrmann's dresser and crashed to the floor several feet away. In its flight, it had knocked over a picture, scarred the mirror frame, and knocked over a lamp. That evening around six, Jimmy was in the rumpus room section of the basement doing his homework when a loud crash— and a yell from Jimmy—brought the family and the reporter on the run. In perhaps the most dramatic feat so far, the children's phonograph, which had been standing on a table by one wall, had sailed across the basement, hit the stairway, and crashed to the cement floor with its case broken.

Ninety minutes later, while the reporter, a policeman, and one of two parapsychologists who had come to study the case were in the basement examining the broken phonograph, a loud noise was heard in the master bedroom. Mrs. Herrmann's night lamp was found overturned on her dresser. Next, Jimmy rushed in to report that a plate of bread standing on the dining room table had fallen to the floor. Although Jimmy had been sitting at the table alone, he said he had not seen the plate actually fall but had only heard the crash. Nevertheless, since the boy had been alone during both this and the phonograph event, suspicion began to refocus on him as the perpetrator.

Then, oddly, all major disturbances abruptly ceased for three days. Even so, Tozzi and his associates still pressed for a physical solution to the case. On the day of the bread plate event, the fire department had checked a well on the front lawn, on the theory that changes in the water table below ground might have something to do with "Popper's" activity. Yet no change was found over the last five years. A report from the town engineer revealed that no underground streams were present. An RCA test truck checked for unusual radio frequencies outside the house; none was discovered. A town inspector had been over every inch of the house and found it structurally sound. The plumbing was checked for unusual vibrations and slight ones were found. But one of the neighboring houses had them too—much louder ones—yet it had no poltergeist. Early in March, nearby Mitchell Air Force Base was asked for a list of departure times of jet aircraft, to see whether any correlation could be found between takeoffs and the disturbances. None could.

Then on March 2, a Sunday, fresh incidents broke out in the afternoon and evening. At this time the Herrmanns had some friends and relatives in the house; one of these saw the glass centerpiece rise from the dining room table and fall to the floor. Later, James Herrmann's bedroom lamp was found overturned. At seven thirty, Jimmy, his father, and an uncle went to the store; when they returned, they found the boy's globe of the world in the middle of his bed. One local newspaper had implied that Jimmy could have caused all the events himself. And once that evening James Herrmann flatly accused his son again, urging him to admit his guilt without further delay. Driven to tears, Jimmy pleaded, "Dad, I had nothing to do with any of it." Hearing her brother cry, Lucille too burst into tears, and so did their mother. Everyone in the house was now living on raw nerve, just waiting for the next calamity.

After the children were put to bed, more things happened

in the unhappy household. Loud crashes from Jimmy's room revealed that the picture over his bed had fallen again. Later, another crash brought Herrmann on the run to his son's room. This time, flashlight in hand, he personally witnessed the night table twist about ninety degrees and topple over. Herrmann's doubts about his son's guilt must have vanished then and there, for the boy was lying quietly in bed looking badly frightened.

During the rest of that week, "Popper" gave the Herrmanns little peace. On Tuesday a reporter from the *London Evening News*—proof in itself of how the poltergeist's reputation was growing—was standing in the living room doorway. Suddenly he saw a photographer's flashbulb, which had been lying on an end table, sail across the entire room and pop to pieces against the opposite wall. A few minutes later, a bottle of Clorox was found in the cellar without its cap, its contents spilling. Jimmy was in the bathroom when one of the most destructive events of all took place. Everyone heard a resounding crash and, rushing into the dining room, found that the glass centerpiece had again smashed into the corner cabinet. This time it had broken off a scalloped wooden portion of it. Minutes later, a heavy bookcase in the cellar toppled over. And so it went, day after day for the whole week.

Both of the parapsychologists, who had been studying the manifestations for several days, were present during the finale of the case. On Sunday, March 9, when both children were in bed, one of the researchers and James Herrmann were talking in the dining room when both heard a cavernous thump from the direction of the boy's room. A search turned up nothing. Three-quarters of an hour later, an even louder thump was heard by everyone. Again nothing was found amiss. Later, the two researchers and Jimmy tried to duplicate the sound by striking various walls, but they could never quite match the original tone qualities.

On March 10, a Monday evening, James Herrmann stayed in New York City to appear on a radio program—the first of several during which he and his family told of their unnerving experiences. In so doing, he missed the last appearance of "Popper," which occurred a few minutes after eight. Everyone was in the upper portion of the house when a loud thump was heard in the basement. It was found that once again, as perhaps befitting the nickname given the poltergeist, a bottle of bleach minus its unscrewed cap was emptying out its liquid on the cement floor.

Jimmy's father soon relinquished his suspicions that Jimmy was responsible for the poltergeist activity. He had a new theory, and years after the events he was quoted as still believing it. Herrmann had become convinced that a type of radio radiation from a submarine navigation station off the Atlantic Coast had somehow caused the phenomena. But the two parapsychologists thought differently. Having ruled out fraud or hoax, psychological considerations, and purely physical causes, they cautiously suggested that *psychokinesis*— that aspect of extrasensory perception popularly known as "mind over matter"—*may* have been at work.

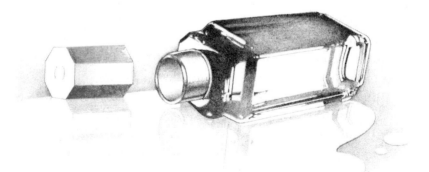

j133.1 Knight, David C.

The moving coffins

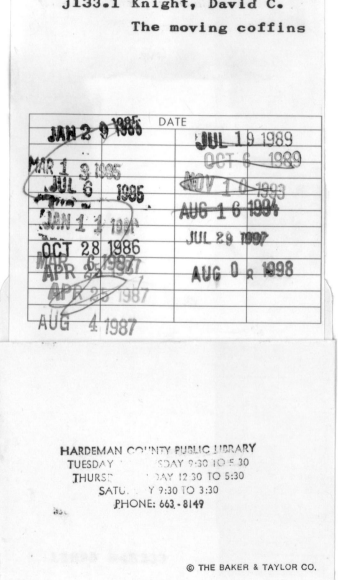

DATE	
JAN 2 0 1985	JUL 1 9 1989
MAR 1 3 1985	OCT 6 1989
JUL 6 1985	NOV 1 0 1993
JAN 1 1 1986	AUG 1 6 1994
OCT 28 1986	JUL 29 1997
MAR 6 1987	
APR 2 1987	AUG 0 8 1998
APR 2 3 1987	
AUG 4 1987	